NARCISSISTIC MOTHERS

A practical guide for Daughter and Son to recognize a Narcissistic Parent Abuse and how to heal and recover from CPTSD

(Complex Post-Traumatic Stress Disorder)

Rose Mary Parker

Narcissistic Mothers

Narcissistic Mothers

TABLE OF CONTENTS

Narcissistic Mothers

Narcissistic Mothers

Introduction

A mother is our route of entry into the world. For many of us, the first breath and first feeling of genuine love come from our mother. The connection we build with her is immediate, as our little bodies automatically get drawn to the sense of protection and love she oozes.

Typically, mothers are perfect for their children, and they even sacrifice their happiness to ensure their kids get the best. They may have their troubles, scars, and needs, but they always find a way to compromise. Even if she gets angry or says things she doesn't mean to her kids, she finds a way to apologize and make it up to them. This is how the love of a good mother is supposed to be, and what kids need for a healthy life.

For some of us, our mothers embody fear and rage. They hurl abuses and never seem to care for our needs. These mothers don't signify safety; neither are they self-sacrificing. Only her needs are a priority. She never comes to a compromise with us, and if we fail to do what she wants, nagging, guilt-tripping, and abuses are her weapons. In the end, she leaves behind a ton of negative emotional baggage in the lives of her kids, who never seem to get over it even as adults. This type of mother is a narcissistic mother.

If this is your story, then you are not alone. Numerous people go through this. Growing up with a narcissistic mother is a challenge, unlike any other. When a narcissistic mother raises you, you experience unexplainable pressure from inside the relationship, outside of the relationship, and inside of yourself. This pressure commands you to be a certain person, a person who can shape-shift into any position that your narcissistic mother requires of you, even when she is not present to see it happen.

The following chapters describe the conditions of narcissism among mothers by making it understandable and bearable. You will be guided on how to take direct action and make a substantial recovery, especially if you have experienced a narcissistic parentage.

I am an empathetic person, and I have a master's in NLP. Due to my previous experience with Narcissistic people in my family, and later in my relationship, I have decided to talk about this hidden subject with you to show you that you are not alone. Talking and recognizing the problem is the first step for healing. I usually interview people, so in this book, you will find cases of daughters and sons of Narcissistic Mothers. You will find real-life instances that may relate to your situations and experience. The self-centered pattern of narcissistic mothers makes them arrogant and lacking other people's compassion and regard. Therefore, you will need an in-depth analysis of issues that arise from experience and how to live positively after that.

With this book, you will learn everything you need to know about breaking free from narcissistic mothers and healing from such effects. You will learn about yourself and how to interact with a narcissistic mother without ruining the mother-daughter relationship.

Thank you again for choosing Narcissistic Mothers. I hope you will find useful information about your awareness and life changing. I would appreciate hearing your thoughts with a short review on Amazon.

Thank you for choosing Narcissistic Mothers. I hope you will find useful information about your awareness and life changing. I would appreciate hearing your thoughts with a short review on Amazon.

PART ONE: NARCISSISM

Chapter 1: Origin of Narcissism

Narcissism is a term that was coined by Paul Nacke in 1899 to refer to someone that was treated as an object. This term was taken up by Freud, and he went ahead to bring up more information about it.

Since this time, the concept of narcissism has grown over borders, and thoughts and theories have come up to make it part of our daily lives. Many people use the word to refer to personal vanity – the desire to make ourselves look better than anyone else.

Just like any other personality disorder, this condition shows a never-ending pattern of behavior that affects the social, professional, and familial relationships of the one suffering from it. These people have an inflated opinion of their perceived abilities or traits. Narcissism makes people feel even more egoistic as they gain the Admiration and praise of other people. Many of them often show that they are superior, but others know how to hide it under acts of pretentious humility. But this is usually ruined when they get criticized. They typically respond by showing rage or making condescending remarks toward the person who offended them with criticism.

People who are suffering from narcissistic personality disorder show sure signs of selfishness; They don't know the meaning of empathy, although some of them may pretend to show it. Some narcissists who have become experts at hiding their disorder may look like they are very generous, understanding, and selfless. But this behavior usually doesn't last.

Narcissism usually develops in early childhood. It seems the emotional trauma responsible for narcissism occurs around the age of a toddler. Hence the narcissist's ability to handle emotions gets stuck at that level of mental development. That explains their dangerous emotional immaturity, doesn't it?

We all get exposed to trauma during the early stages of our development. It's only inevitable. Injury can result from something as simple as not being picked up by our parent as a baby or being fed against our will. It could also result from something more severe, as our mother left us at the kindergarten for the first time, which can cause a long-lasting fear of separation. Our parents fighting and screaming at each other in our presence can leave their imprints on our subconscious mind, too. So, what kind of trauma produces a narcissist?

Growing up with an either overbearing and completely neglectful parent can warp a child's mind and cause them to be narcissistic adults later in life. A parent can be overbearing when it comes to a child's performance in school and neglectful when it comes to a child's emotional needs.

The trauma of a narcissist is the perceived lack of control. The inability to acknowledge their own emotions makes a narcissist extremely uncomfortable.

Admitting one "wrong" thing about themselves would make them feel as though everything is wrong. So, every abusive and manipulative action they take only serves one purpose: to feel in control. The root of their toxic behavior towards you has nothing to with you, and it has everything to do with them. If you play close attention to their accusations, you will see that they, in fact, project their behavior, fears, and doubts on you. A narcissist may often lie, yet accuse you of lying all the time, no matter how much proof you present that they are wrong.

You must keep in mind that narcissists never truly learned how to express and process their emotions. Their parents may have been overly protective and proud of them – but only when they fulfilled their parents' expectations. One could try to do some research about the past of the narcissist in question. Though it usually is challenging to get a clear picture. It's complicated to find the truth about a narcissist, especially when their parents admit to not having been able to handle their child.

In many cases, one or both of their parents may display some narcissistic traits, too. That does not mean, however, that the children of a narcissist are bound to become narcissistic as well.

This can be an environmental cause that can lead to a forced image of perfection later in life. Another aspect is early childhood abuse. One way to deal with abuse is to see yourself as above it, too clean for it. Taking an abusive history into account, narcissism acts as a wall to prevent being hurt further in the future. Despite the several ways the disorder can be environmental, there is also some belief that the trait can, in fact, be hereditary. With genetics, though, seeing a specific behavioral feature can be difficult. Often, though it may seem genetic, it is moreover the way that parent or grandparent was raised that gives them the condition. This brings up the question of actual genetics. Science has yet to come to a clear conclusion on that, though. Studies have not been able to go to a solid end, and with many different conditions, it is hard to see which is environmental and which is genetic.

The majority of the cases of Narcissistic Personality Disorder, though, always points back to the parents who raised the child. Whether it is neglect, abuse, overprotection, rewarding for insignificance, Munchausen, or even the parent giving the child a hypochondriac disorder or a sense that they are superior, the child's behavior is usually created at an early age. With such a deep-seated basis and such a long time for growth, this makes the disorder even harder to overcome later in life. Changing someone's perspective of how they should see the world when they were raised and to see it differently can be a nearly impossible task. This also can cause more behavioral and personality issues. Taking away the one or only defense someone has constructed to deal with trauma can then lead to an exposed and vulnerable feeling that can cause depression and anxiety. What happens then is the person goes from being narcissistic to high-risk Avoidant Personality Disorder, agoraphobia, social anxiety, self-harm, and even suicidal, or an intention of hurting others. People using narcissism to cover an abusive or traumatic childhood would have to be approached with the utmost care.

Even if the issues are genetic, there is really no direct way to treat genetics over a learned behavior cycle.

Hereditary behavior issues are something a species line has evolved to. Somehow that series of genetics has evolved into seeing itself as more significant than others. Whether this has to do with the biological mating habits or some kind of protective reaction of the line, it is part of who the person is. Just as someone is likely to have a stronger inclination to be a leader or one who helps people for a living, being someone who sees themselves as above others will already be in their head from early childhood. As with learned behavior, this comes from one or both parents. If the parent(s) has the same genetic disposition, then they will raise the child with that frame of mind, once again, the person is locked in a cycle. Being both genetically superior and raised to believe that they are so will be the prime persona of the person and thus something which is not easy to change.

Notes:

_____
_____
_____
_____
_____
_____
_____
_____
_____
_____
_____
_____
_____
_____
_____
_____
_____
_____
_____
_____
_____
_____
_____
_____
_____
_____
_____
_____
_____

Narcissistic Mothers

Narcissistic Mothers

Chapter 2: Identifying a Narcissist

You know that work colleague or friend who always manages to be at the center of attention, making everything to be about them. What about that family member who is in the habit of demeaning everyone because they believe they are smarter than everybody else?

Interacting with a narcissist can be daunting, and that's why it is essential to be able to identify their dominating character traits. The truth is that they are no physical body tests that one can perform to ascertain the presence of narcissism. But it is possible to observe certain behavior and reactions and identify this condition.

An inflated sense of self-importance

They believe that they are exceptional and unusual and can only interact with others "unique." In other words, they are too good for anything ordinary or average and only want to associate with other high-ranking people, places or things

They will exaggerate their achievements and capabilities and make everyone feel how lucky they are to have them in their lives. They are the undisputed heroes, and everyone else ranks second in their hierarchy.

A sense of entitlement and preeminence

Because of their overestimated sense of importance, narcissists expect favorable treatment whenever they go. They consider themselves unique and believe that they should get everything they want. They expect everyone around them to be at their beck and call and comply with their every wish and whim. If you don't comply and meet their every need, then the term you as useless.

Unrealistic need for praise and Admiration

Narcissists' sense of grandiose is like a balloon that needs a constant supply of air to keep it inflated. Likewise, their ego requires a steady source of applause and validation to keep it inflated. The occasional compliment does not count, and that's why they surround themselves with people who are willing to feed their ego with words of affirmation and praise continually.

These interactions are one-sided as it is always about what the devotee can do to the narcissist and not the other way round. And if there is ever a breach or a reduction of praise and affirmation from the admirer, the narcissist treats that as disloyalty, and the devotee will face dire consequences.

Lives in a perfect world that supports their delusions

Narcissists will dwell in this fantasy bubble, and anything that threatens to burst it is met with extreme range and defensiveness. Facts and opinions that intimidate them are ignored or rationalized, and so those around the narcissist must learn to trend carefully for peace to prevail. They have a warped sense of perception about things around them.

Lack of empathy for other people

Narcissists are not able to identify with the feelings of other people. In other words, they cannot put themselves in other people's shoes but exploit without guilt or shame. To them, the people around them are there to serve their needs and replenish their insatiable thirst for approval.

To that end, they don't think twice about taking advantage of others to achieve their desires. In most cases, this exploitation is glaring, and in these others, it is subtle and hard to be noticed.

Narcissisms don't consider how their manipulative behaviors affect others, and even if you try to point out to them, they simply don't get it. All they think about is how to satisfy their needs and feed their egos.

Meticulousness

Many narcissists have an extremely high sense of perfection. They believe that things should happen exactly as planned, and life should be as they envision it in their minds. This is an impossible demand in the real world, which results in the narcissist feeling miserable and depressed all the time.

Narcissists who are inclined to perfection are very difficult to please. Nothing you do will be right enough, and you are always to meet their infinite needs for Admiration, love, service, or purchases. Failure to meet these desires may lead to dismissal. They cannot take a "no" and often expect others to inconvenience themselves so that they can serve them.

They want to be in control

We have established that most narcissists are perfectionists, and when they feel things are not working out to their stands, they develop this great need to controlling other words. They will do anything possible to be in control of a situation and manipulate it to their liking. With their unreasonably high sense of entitlement, they will demand to control events because they believe it is the logical thing to do. In essence, they have everything figured out in their minds. They have a storyline in mind and have assigned specific roles to each person in that particular set up. If any person behaves contrary, the narcissist becomes very agitated because you have unsettled what was in the script. You are a threat to their desired outcome.

Thrive in the blame game

In most cases, the narcissist will blame the one person who is the most loyal and emotionally attached to them. This dedicated admirer is the safest to blame because the chances of denying or rejecting the blame are very minimal.

Thrill-seekers

Anyone working with a narcissist will find themselves in a roller coaster, swinging in random directions. You will conform to the activity that brings the maximum thrill to the narcissist. When the adrenaline rush hits, strategic plans are thrown out of the window and replaced by reactivity to a self-inflicted crisis. The bottom line is that narcissist is forever chasing thrill because the resulting excitement makes them feel good about themselves. The excitement also serves as an outlet for all the pressure and aggression that is usually bottled up in them.

Extreme sensitivity to criticism

They will attack and hurl all manner of insults to their critics and banish them from their perceived glorious presence. Narcissists will expect their opponents to be devastated when not in their coverage, and this gives them a sense of pride and importance.

Surprisingly, the same people who dread to be criticized are overly critical of other people. They can see their own problems but believe other people are problematic and need to change.

Lack of a sense of humor

Narcissists are too severe in their life. They don't get jokes, and they don't make jokes except for a few sarcastic remarks and weird puns. Their lack of empathy makes them not to grasp the context and emotional aspects of the words, actions, jokes, and humor expressed. For a person to laugh at a joke or make a humorous relevant, he/ she must, first of all, understand the context and effect of the people around him. Narcissists lack this critical concept and consequently specialize in sarcasm, which they mistake for wits.

Have undefined interpersonal boundaries

Narcissists will unconsciously view others as extensions of themselves. They can't tell where they end and where the other person begins. They regard other people as existing solely to serve them and will disregard their needs, family obligations, and any other duty that their loyal followers have to fulfill. They are regarded as 'narcissists supply,' existing mainly to cater to their personal needs, and therefore it is difficult for the narcissist to think of them indecently. They generally expect their devotees to be at their beck and call.

Notes:

_____

_____

_____

_____

_____

_____

_____

_____

_____

_____

_____

_____

_____

_____

_____

_____

_____

_____

_____

_____

_____

_____

_____

_____

_____

Narcissistic Mothers

Chapter 3: What is narcissism?

Narcissism is when you love yourself way more than others. These kinds of individuals give priority to their desires and needs over anyone else's. They care about nobody except themselves. People who showcase this behavior are known as narcissists.

You can notice narcissism in different kinds of individuals, including coworkers, spouses, family members, and friends. The boss who always undermines you at work regardless of what you do can be a narcissist. It could also be your parent who makes you feel less for refusing to do their bidding.

Narcissists can also channel most of their efforts into being the best they can be in the eyes of the public. They thrive on attention and enjoy it when others are envious of them, even though they exhibit unhealthy behaviors to people they live with.

They are charming enough to attract people to like them, to make them think that they are amazing. It is common for them to make prospects fall in love so they can be their true narcissistic selves without the risk of being abandoned.

Narcissism is a character trait in which someone displays a heightened over-confidence due to their Admiration of themselves; they can simply do no wrong. This is an exaggerated behavior that breathes and exudes arrogance, pretentiousness, and a deep-rooted ideology of false superiority. "I am special. Everyone else in the world is below me because they are not me". A person who exhibits narcissistic characteristics is often described as being cocky, self-centered, self-absorbed, and rude. They view life as a playground for manipulating emotion, as an untapped market in which to exploit and to bend the truth at will. They can be considered to be "winners," but they are crude people to be involved with due to their self-described perfection. So, too, are they, liars. Their success – in most cases – is because of their total and complete disregard for other people and their feelings. Or rather, narcissists will push past people no matter what those people are feeling. They view other people as obstacles. We are their next hurdle to get over. They would most likely push us off the edge of a top-floor balcony if it meant that they would get just a little more ahead of everyone else.

Narcissists are the perennial interrupters of conversation. They continuously crave the limelight; they feel as if they deserve everyone's attention at every single turn. They want to be seen. They want to be heard. They want to be the leading figure in any small gathering, work circles, friendship circles, and among the large crowds. They are the people who ooze confidence in every moment. They are very charming people, and more often than not, they are quite funny, very sarcastic. They are an excellent company in public. Still, once at home and in their respective comfort zones, they shed their beautiful skins for the emotionally deprived, ostentatious colors that they don't have when returned to their private and intimate places. They use manipulation and excessive, yet believable, lies as a tool to such an extent that narcissists are almost fanatical individuals regarding their use of such methods.

Narcissists have such a deep self-belief burning within them. But beneath all of that lies a person who has been deeply affected by life. Narcissists are people, though pretty hardcore ones, who have been shaped by past trauma, past experiences, or past abuse. Narcissism has crafted them into a person with such anxiety that the line between nervousness and abandonment has morphed and blurred into a singularly individualistic focus. The Admiration that they are continually seeking is due to their inner mental conflicts that were borne from a lonely and possibly unloved childhood. This has made them develop what we could call external spotlighted arrogance. The definition of this is, simply, a spotlight. Some form of the inner spotlight that externalizes itself – or switches on - when it feels like it needs to be seen, it burns so bright that it forces people to shift and focus all undivided attention on the narcissist. This trait, or behavioral characteristic, if looked at from a psychological perspective, is most common in children below the age of 10. It is that you need to stand out from the rest, to get attention, whether that is from your parents, your family, your friends. It's a phase our brains go through during early childhood development that can be best linked to the behavior-type of somebody that wants to brag about something. In a narcissist's case, what they are mostly bragging about is themselves.

We all know a narcissist. They could be our mother or our father; they could have been this way for as long as we can remember and have left us, now in adulthood, shattered, confused, exhausted. They could be our brother or our sister. They were always showered with praise, always told that they were the star – they were serial winners and developed an egotism that has become the prospective difficulties in our lives, still affecting us at this very moment. They could be a work colleague or employee. But what are the roots of narcissism?

Narcissists tend to view themselves quite differently when compared to others, and they often make those around them feel inadequate and devalued. Here's the kicker—a narcissist always wants everything to be about themselves. You might not mind showering a one-year-old infant with all your attention, but you will start to mind when a 35-year-old demands the same level of care and achieves it at your expense.

Narcissists easily victimize others by just being who they are, and it is unlikely they will ever change. This might seem rather severe, but until you deal with a narcissist, you will not realize how toxic, such individuals can be. To understand NPD, you must first understand the way narcissists think about themselves.

Narcissists are often characterized by high self-worth. This characteristic affects the thoughts and behaviors of an individual, as well as his interaction with others.

Narcissism is considered normal up to a certain extent. When it gets to the extreme, it turns into a disorder(NPD). A person that is full of himself, and one finds it difficult to appreciate others, can be considered as a narcissist. Narcissism is also evident in individuals who love too much attention and those who exercise a high sense of superiority. Some people call it self-centredness or self-love.

It is always easy to identify a narcissistic person in a group of people. Such individuals always hype the crowd and keep sharing stories about themselves. They always seem to be more interested in their success. Narcissists tend to be manipulated and often lack a sense of compassion. Other traits associated with this personality include:

- A crave for appreciation and acknowledgment even when nothing has been accomplished

- Appreciation of personal beauty and success

- A feeling of being better than others

- Exploit and manipulation of others

- Grandiosity and a high emphasis on self

- Fantasies of being critical, famous or influential

- Exaggeration of individual accomplishments and abilities

Notes:

_____

_____

_____

_____

_____

_____

_____

_____

_____

_____

_____

_____

_____

_____

_____

_____

_____

_____

_____

_____

_____

_____

_____

_____

Narcissistic Mothers

Chapter 4: Narcissistic Strategies of Manipulation

Narcissistic mothers are never logical. They never agree they are wrong and often throw tantrums when you try to call them out on their behavior. Most times, they try to manipulate you to get their way. These manipulation techniques are very subtle and can be challenging to spot. However, to properly ensure you don't fall for their antics, you need to learn to spot them.

In this section, we will be looking into some of the ways a narcissistic mother tries to manipulate and how you can protect yourself.

Emotional Blackmail

Here the narcissistic mother seems to appeal to you for something. However, in reality, this is not an appeal but a demand, and if you refuse to do it, then you face a barrage of consequences. All of these are to ensure you agree to her request. If you fail to do what she wants, she will capitalize on many of the weapons in her arsenal to punish you. She will throw insults, give you the cold shoulder, withdraw affection and love, and even threaten you with physical violence. These are some forms of emotional abuse the narcissistic parent uses to control you.

For instance: Your narcissistic mother may request that you leave all of your prior engagements and come for a program that is important to her. Because her proposed commitment is impromptu, and you already made plans way beforehand, you tell her you won't be able to make it along with your reasons.

Instead of trying to understand your perspectives and respecting your desires, she goes ahead to tell you how ungrateful you are for not being there when she needs you. If you still refuse to show up, she gives you the cold shoulder for weeks, or even months.

How to protect yourself: Set up boundaries and know the extent of these boundaries. You are allowed to reject any request or invitation if it does not fit your schedule. This becomes particularly important when dealing with a person who has toxic behavior. You have the right to reject requests. Refuse to fall for any cold shoulders or insults that may come your way.

If you live far away from your narcissistic mother, an easier way is to keep your distance. Ensure you don't respond to text messages or emails they send to guilt-trip you. Say no and stand your ground no matter what happens.

She Uses Obligation and Fear to Guilt-Trip You

It is not strange for narcissistic parents to use fear and obligation to guilt-tip you into doing their bidding even if it does not align with your desires.

For instance: Your mother is the owner of a renowned company, and she wants you to take the mantle. However, you have other plans for your life, and when you tell her you are happier doing something else, she lashes out and says, "What is going to happen to our family legacy? Is this how you want to repay me for all the sacrifices I made for you? You are a shame to the family, and you don't deserve our name!"

How to protect yourself: When a narcissist parent guilt trips, you understand that any shame or guilt that comes from it is not genuine. Remember that it is your right to have preferences and make choices, even if your narcissistic mother does not support these choices. You don't need to explain to anyone about the options you make in your personal life, especially when they are only after their benefit..

Shaming

Narcissistic parents shame their kids to make them feel less about themselves. According to research, when a person feels imperfect and flawed, they are more likely to acquiesce to the demands of others. This is why it is a useful tool when in the hands of a narcissistic parent. They shame you with your personal information, whether publicly or privately, to make you more compliant with their desires.

For instance: Your narcissistic mother starts to make snide comments about your choice of a partner during your family Christmas gathering. Even though your marriage is a successful one, and you are happy with your partner, they keep poking at your areas of imperfection all because you did not marry the woman they chose for you. They may continuously tell you how your marriage is going to fail and how you both won't make good parents.

How to protect yourself: Don't let your mother continuous with this behavior. Try to keep the distance, and you will not show up as much for any events they will be part of. Instead of dwelling in shame, remember how far you have come, and how happy you are. Instead of being ashamed of yourself, acknowledge your areas of success, and take pride in them.

She Compares

We covered comparison earlier on. Narcissistic parents often compare their kids to others to make them feel less.

For example: Your childhood friend comes over and tells you he just got a new well-paying job. Later on, your mother asks you why you can't be more like your childhood friend, and also proceeds to ask what you are doing with your life.

How to protect yourself: You need to remember that all humans are different in areas they excel in. Do not let anyone draw you in with comparisons. Note that this is another strategy to make you feel less, and if you fall for it, you will only be making your narcissist parent win over you.

Instead of trying to make your mother understand by listing out your achievements, don't bother. This is because she would still find a way to make them worthless anyway. You should channel your time and energy into hanging around people that support you and understand the value of what you have achieved. Don't compare yourself with other people to feel successful.

Notes:

_____

_____

_____

_____

_____

_____

_____

_____

_____

_____

_____

_____

_____

_____

_____

_____

_____

_____

_____

_____

_____

_____

_____

_____

_____

_____

_____

_____

_____

Narcissistic Mothers

Chapter 5: How a Narcissist can control you

Dealing with a narcissist means that every day could be a challenge. However, it helps if you know what to expect from them, so you won't end up disappointed.

A narcissist does not have any respect for you and your boundaries. They might even encourage talks against you, gossips about you, and fools you into believing that he or she is in love with you.

Promises are made to be broken, all the time. Narcissists make them, but will likely not honor them. When you confront them about it, they would vehemently deny it. They might even feel indignant by saying how dare you for thinking that they did something wrong by forgetting their promise. They might even blame you and your "high standards" for the fact that they failed to realize their promise.

A narcissist will only do something if they know they can get something out of it. They won't mow the lawn, wash the dishes, or run errands for you if they know that these things will not get appreciated or rewarded for it. They always want to be credited for everything that they do. If it goes unnoticed, prepare to listen to their ranting about it.

Humility is definitely out of reach, and their priority will always be themselves. They are not even ashamed of being selfish and feeling entitled.

They do not recognize boundaries. Narcissists are used to crossing personal boundaries if it means getting to their goal. It could be to hurt you or another person, and they won't apologize for it.

Narcissists are not capable of loving and caring. They do have feelings, but these are all based on certain conditions. Usually, they will show the motions of loving you if they know that you can boost their ego by supporting their grandiose view of themselves. If you disagree with them, then don't expect them to show their fake love and warmth.

The narcissist lives to trigger emotional reactions in people because, in their minds, that gives them some sense of power. If a narcissist causes you to lose control over your emotions, it gives him a lot of satisfaction. When a narcissist attacks you verbally, ignoring him can drive him crazy.

You have to understand that narcissists crave attention, so ignoring them hurts them more than anything else. They want to be acknowledged and validated; that is why they start with the conflict in the first place. When a narcissist targets you and destroys your life, your natural instinct will be to get back at him/her by reacting angrily and emotionally, but if you do that, you are only playing into his/her hand.

It may not seem so at first. Still, over time, you will realize that ignoring the narcissist is much more satisfying than engaging with him/her because then, even to third-party observers, the narcissist will just seem like a petty person who likes to pick fights with people. You will look like a mature adult who can rise above it all.

The narcissist wants to control you and to assert dominance over you, but you have to remember that people can't take power from you. You have to give it to them. A narcissist can only dominate you if you relinquish control to him/her. As we have mentioned, you are guaranteed to lose if you play the narcissist's game, and that is when he/she is capable of dominating you. By ignoring the narcissist, you blatantly refuse to perform his/her game, and then he/she has no means with which to get close enough to have any form of control over your life.

Notes:

_____

_____

_____

_____

_____

_____

_____

_____

_____

_____

_____

_____

_____

_____

_____

_____

_____

_____

_____

_____

_____

_____

_____

_____

_____

_____

Narcissistic Mothers

Chapter 6: Manipulation technique

Gaslighting is one of the most effective standard tool narcissists use. It includes narcissistic parents too. This is a kind of emotional abuse where the mother continuously makes up stories to distort the reality of the victim, which is the child in this case.

Soon, the victim begins to be unsure of his or her instincts and would completely believe the reality of the abuser, even if the child has proof of these answers.

Calling out the toxic parent for their behavior becomes impossible with gaslighting as the victim will be conditioned to believe they are the toxic ones if they do. Victims of gaslighting have a higher probability of dealing with other kinds of abuse, as well.

For instance: Your narcissistic mother asks you to do something for her that would result in you going out of your way. You tell her why this would be impossible as you already have a lot on your plate. Rather than understanding and respecting your wishes, she continues to push and pester you to do her bidding. When you still fail to comply, she goes ahead to punish you with snide comments and insults, even in the presence of others.

The next day when you believe the situation must have calmed down, you try to call her out on her behavior the day before. Instead of admitting and apologizing her wrong, she responds with, "You are over-reacting, I never insulted you. Perhaps you are creating events in your mind."

If, in any case, you try to encounter her about something she has done, she insults you telling you that you have a vivid imagination. This is common across all sorts of narcissists to invalidate your experience over your abuse. She also abuses you that she can't understand what you are talking about. She pretends to forget about very memorable events denying like it never happened, and when you remind her, she does not admit of any possibility that she might have forgotten. This tactic is referred to as "gaslighting," and entails a very aggressive and exceptionally infuriating behavior that is common across all sorts of narcissists. She undermines your perceptions of reality, which kills your confidence in your reasoning power, your memory, and intuition, which makes you a complete victim to her.

Moreover, narcissistic mothers are always gaslight. You will hear them telling you that you are unstable to listen to certain things. They refer to you as over-reactive, completely unreasonable, hysterical, always imagining, or oversensitive.

Once she has constructed these false fantasies of your emotional pathologies, she will share them with others, showing them how helpless and a victim she is with you around her. She always claims to be innocent and states that she ultimately doesn't understand why you are so angry with her. You end up being the one who hurt her and thinks that you need psychotherapy. She claims how much she loves and cares about you and would do anything to see you happy, but she doesn't understand how. According to her, all you do is pushing her when all she wanted was to help you. She complains that she has sacrificed her responsibilities for your empathy and concludes that something is wrong about you. She uses this as a weapon to undermine your credibility with her listeners by clearly elaborating how perfect she plays her role as a mother.

How to Protect Yourself: Individuals who suffer from gaslighting tend to doubt everything and hardly do anything by themselves. This goes on until adulthood. As opposed to allowing yourself to be conditioned, don't give in. Remember that everything your narcissistic parent wants you to believe is not the truth. Find your reality and hold on to it.

To ensure you don't forget, keeping a journal at this point would be a great idea. Anytime your parent abuses you, write it down so you can remember the original version even when they try to gaslight you later on. Do not live by the reality your narcissistic parent tries to plant. If you do, you would be less likely to prevent yourself from being exploited.

No one deserves to be exposed to emotional abuse or manipulation of any form. Stand your ground and resist it as much as you can.

Notes:

Narcissistic Mothers

PART TWO: TRAITS OF NARCISSISTIC MOTHERS

Chapter 1 : Test to recognize your narcissistic mother

Ask yourself the following questions to recognize if your mother is a narcissist. I decide to avoid any score or final ranking. The scope of the test is to allow you to take some time to think, preferably in a quiet place, and to talk with yourself. The answer will come. It is there, in some hidden part of your heart.

Does your mother Deny Everything?

Even if people realize they are lying or denying involvement, a narcissist will continue to do whatever necessary to act like they did nothing wrong. As a child, you were often blamed for what your mother did. This is because you were the most natural target to use since you were less likely to argue or speak the truth to avoid receiving her wrath. Furthermore, most children want to protect their parents, just as their parents are supposed to protect them. Even if you didn't receive protection from your mother, you still felt the urge to protect her.

Is your mother Oblivious?

They have no idea they have a mental illness and are unaware of the impact their behavior has on others. This can make it very difficult to treat narcissists and also makes it nearly impossible for them to have healthy relationships with other people. All of their interaction with the other people in their lives is focused on themselves, making the continuation of any kind of favorable two-way relation that they start extremely difficult for the other person.

Does your mother Lack of Appropriate Emotion?

The narcissist cannot feel appropriate relational emotions because their life is not about others ... it's only about them. So not only do they not have normal love emotions, but they also either repress totally or never really feel emotions like regret when they should. After hurting someone else emotionally, even committing acts of violence, when they should feel shame and remorse, they do not. They live a life never apologizing, asking for forgiveness, or for that matter, even feeling bad about hurting other people emotionally or physically.

Is your mother a braggart?

They are braggarts to the extreme. Their bragging can be subtle and crafty so as not to be visible and blatant about it, attempting to avoid getting caught in exaggerations. They can become very good at the "skill" of bragging. The bragging will be determined and unrelenting. If they do have provable achievements, they will always exaggerate the importance of the accomplishments they can prove.

Does your Mother Lie to You?

Narcissists are known to lie. They do this to manipulate or control you to get what they want. They will also lie to themselves. They need to do this to make themselves look better in front of other people. Many narcissists are believed to be compulsive liars, but this isn't necessarily true. Narcissists usually know when they are lying, whereas compulsive liars don't always understand they are lying.

Is your mother Manipulative?

One of the most significant traits of a narcissist is they are manipulative. A narcissist will use various manipulation tactics to gain control of the situation. For example, your mother negatively compares you to one of your siblings, shames or embarrasses you when you don't comply with what she wants or says you are ungrateful and don't care about her.

Does She use comparison as her major putdowns?

She keeps talking about how someone else did something unusual on the same thing you did, and the contrast is aimed up to you. She ensures that you are no good without even saying a word and spoil your pleasure by congratulating you in an unhappy, envious, and angry voice, making you feel useless. She is completely deniable. Even though it is always possible to confront someone by observing their facial expressions, the way they look at you, and their tone of voice, the case for a narcissistic mother is different. She makes sure you fully understand the punishment that will follow immediately if you object any of her opinions, which makes you afraid, feeling that you are always wrong, but you can't point out why.

Does She violate your boundaries?

You always feel like you are an extension of her. She always gives out your property without even asking, sometimes even in front of you, and when you complain, she will confront you that it was never even yours. She expresses opinions that were meant to be yours and commit your time without also consulting you. She discusses you while present as if you are not there. She doesn't respect your privacy; she storms into your bedroom or bathroom with or without your consent. She keeps asking nosy questions, snoops into your conversations, diary, letters, and email. She is always digging into your feelings, especially if they are harmful and can be used against you.

Does she undermine?

She can only acknowledge the accomplishments of her children if she is capable of taking credit for them. However, if they don't benefit her, she diminishes or ignores all the achievements or successes. Whenever you are at the stage, and she can't get a chance to be the center of attention, she responds negatively by trying to prevent the occasion altogether. She misses the event; she leaves the occasion early; she acts as if it is not a big deal, or even leave a negative comment that someone else did better than you.

Does she denigrate, criticize, and demean?

A narcissistic mother makes sure that you are aware of all the little things. She thinks less of you as compared to what she does to other people or your siblings in general. If, in any case, you complain about mistreatment by someone else, she immediately takes the other person's position to attack you even if she knows nothing about the other person. She never acknowledges your complaints or about those people's justices. All she cares about is to make you feel that you are never right.

Does she use Codependency to Control You?

Many children feel they can never live their own life because their mother is always saying, "I can't live with you, so don't leave me." While most parents don't want their children to grow up and leave them, they know it is inevitable and a part of life. They also feel this is a bittersweet moment as they are proud of their children for accomplishing milestones such as going off to college, getting their first full-time job, and buying their own home. Narcissists don't feel the same way. They need their children with them, even if they don't act like it, because it's the only way they can ensure control over you. If you leave their home or move away, they can no longer hold power over you.

Does She React Extremely When Criticized?

Narcissism is where an individual would easily make fun of someone or criticize everything, but get so mad when the same is done to them. It helps people inflate their egos beyond normal, as they are in love with an ideal self and not the real self.

Is she always envious?

Whenever you get something right, she gets envious and angry, which only disappears if she loves whatever it is that makes you successful. If not, she will make attempts to spoil it for you, take it from you or get the same but better for herself. She always makes sure that she is on the right track to understanding what other people have. Narcissistic mothers envy goes way far to even competing sexually with their daughters or daughters-in-law. They are actively forbidding them to groom themselves or even wear make-up while also criticizing their looks. The envy can also extend to relationships where the narcissist mother interferes with their children's marriage and the upbringing of their grandchildren.

Is she always the center of attention all the time?

Children are the source of adoration and attention for narcissistic mothers. More often, you find yourself doing some chores in the most appropriate time just because she sees you there. You find that something you didn't have to do that day or that week, you have to do it on her demand. She opts to be the entertainer so that she can be the life of her party and will make attempts to distract or spoil when someone else drags the attention, especially if it's the moment of her scapegoat child. She always invites herself during moments when she is not welcome. When either of you pay a visit, she requires you to spend the time with her and entertaining her is endless. When you happen to do something without involving her, deprived her attention, or refused to wait for her on something, she ends up being raged, manipulated, or even pouted.

Does she manipulate your emotions to feed on your pain?

The extraordinarily bizarre and sick behavior is typical among almost all sorts of narcissistic mothers that their children always refer to them as emotional vampires. Sadism is one of the strategies used to feed these emotions to the children. The narcissistic mother is actively needling you about the things you are sensitive to, and she keeps saying or doing things just to wound you. She engages herself in a tormenting teasing manner, but shortly, you would see a smile over her lips.

Is your mother willful and selfish?

A narcissistic mom will always ensure that she wins the best of Everything. She follows and believes in her ways and will pursue it manipulatively and ruthlessly even if it will cost her some extra efforts or going past the normal behavior. She makes enormous efforts to win something you denied her also if you were right about her not having it, or she demanded it unreasonably and selfishly.

Does she Lack Insight?

Manipulative mothers don't know how to engage with people, and to this end, they create specific scenarios that will absolve them of any responsibility. They believe that the only way to handle a situation between them, you, or their husband is to make sure their needs are met. This is all that matters in the relationship with other people.

Does she Talk Ill About Others?

If you want to know the real intention of the Manipulative mother, and then pay attention to the way they talk about other people about what you do for them. What they tell you about other people is what they will tell others about you.

Does she Pretend to Listen?

You will at first think that she is an excellent listener and see it as ethical behavior, but what they are after is looking for loopholes in what you are saying so that they can discredit you. They look for the holes so that they can find something to criticize you, and then judge you just to fulfill their egos.

Does she Exaggerate?

Manipulative mothers will find a way to turn around the truth so that it works in their favor.

Even when you realize that they have turned around the fact, they will brush it off in a ginger way and come up with hidden truths in the same words that you said.

Is she always Loud?

They also always think that talking louder makes them look smart in front of other people. They do this all the time. Do you remember when you went for an event, and your mother was the loudest in the room till you became embarrassed?

The loudness is all about trying to push you into submission. You will never be successful if you engage in a shouting match with your narcissistic mother.

Is she Always Negative?

Manipulative mothers aren't happy people, and this reflects through both life and work. They will yell and scream at all people, regardless of their age and status. They might also decide to go silent, and in all this, they are enjoying immensely.

It is because they are unhappy that they want everyone else to share in their unhappiness. When other people are unhappy, they see that they are in full control of the situation, but what they do just ruins the environment for everyone.

Does she Ridicule You?

Manipulative mothers will find any situation to make you feel bad about yourself over something that you have done or accomplished. They will do this in such a way that it isn't as apparent to all people but just you. The negative comment might be something as simple as commenting on your way of dressing, but from experience, you know that they are out to hurt you.

Does your mother Judge Openly?

Manipulative mothers make no apologies when you get offended, and in most cases, will not apologize for saying that they are wrong or they have done something wrong. It might not be the wrong thing for you, but as long as it doesn't please her, then it is illegal in her sight.

Does she Make You Question Your Abilities?

Manipulative mothers will have the expertise to make you doubt your capabilities. They will make you feel silly for doing and saying things, even if they are essential to you. They will also make your feelings seem unimportant at all times.

Does your mother Ignore Your Problems?

Rather than being empathetic when you have an issue, they tend to make it their own. If you are sick, they will come up with the same issue that you have but worse. If you fight with your sibling, they will find a way to turn it around so that they make you look bad in it. Once the mother manipulates you, the effects can be short or long term.

Does your mother regularly shame you?

Narcissistic mothers always use shaming as a weapon to ensure that their children will never develop constant self-esteem or identity to make sure that they will never become independent enough to live without her approval or validation. She publicly shames her children for not achieving much personally, professionally, socially, or even academically. She shames them about their preferences, personality, dressing manner, lifestyle, friends, partner, and career choices.

Notes:

_____
_____
_____
_____
_____
_____
_____
_____
_____
_____
_____
_____
_____
_____
_____
_____
_____
_____
_____
_____
_____
_____
_____
_____
_____
_____
_____
_____
_____
_____

Narcissistic Mothers

Narcissistic Mothers

Chapter 2: Types Of Narcissistic Mothers

The common types of narcissistic parents we have to include:

The Flashy Extrovert

The extrovert mother is one of the most common kinds of narcissistic mothers you will find around. In the eyes of the public, they are entirely perfect, and everyone wants to be like them. Outside, she is fun, easy to notice, and very flashy. If her child can keep up the act out, the better the treatment meted to him or her. If the child can't, he or she will be treated with the cold shoulder.

Only those who live with her know that she is not who she portrays herself to be. Her children will most likely have no love for her because they know she is a pretender. She gives respect to only those who can help her keep up her appearances in the external world. Everyone, including strangers, loves these kinds of narcissistic mothers, except her children, which makes them desperately yearn for her love. In most cases, these mothers have a great social circle that they want to keep intact. For this reason, they force their children to do all they can to fit in by projecting what she wants through them.

For example, Jane's mother is the leader of a prestigious club. They are all about making new connections and proper etiquettes. To belong, you must meet a certain standard in vocabulary, dressing, and appeal. Jane's mother enjoys showing off to other members about how perfect she is. She also tells stories of things that never happened to keep all of the attention on herself. Everything must be accurate, and nothing must dent her image, including her child. If Jane does not want to suffer abuse or her mother's rage, she must also play the role of the perfect daughter once they are out. The instant they are back home, her mother doesn't care anymore.

Anything that does not affect her image positively or negatively is not her concern.

The Accomplishment-Oriented Mothers

To these groups of narcissistic mothers, your achievement in life is her utmost priority. She expects her children to perform their best using the standards she has put in place. Her definition of success and achievement is based on what a person does and not who the person is. If you want the love of this kind of mother, your grades have to be the best; you need to be the top at every game and tournament, get admission to the leading colleges, and get a job with the most prestigious organizations.

These mothers enjoy getting attention by using the accomplishment of their kids. After all, they are her accomplishments too. If you meet up to her standards, you will be showered with love and affection at every turn.

It can be very confusing dealing with this mother because when you put all of the work involved in meeting her standards, you have no support from her. However, the instant you can meet her expectations, you become the apple of her eye. She all smiles when she attends the award ceremonies that happen as a result of your achievements. Children with this type of narcissistic mother soon understand that if they want the attention, love, and support of their mother, they have to be at the top. This may lead the child into a high-achieving lifestyle. Also, they are usually devastated if they fail because they know what comes next.

The Psychosomatic Mothers

This group of mothers enjoys manipulating their children, and they use aches, illnesses, and pains to do it. She uses all of these tools to ensure attention stays on her at all times. She needs to get the priority, and any child who wants to be loved and cared for this mother has to play the role of a caretaker. If you call her out on her behavior or fail to fall for her antics, she gets a health crisis. This usually works in making you feel guilty for failing to be there when your mother needed you the most.

For a narcissistic mother, the only important thing is her child to be at her beck and call, caring for her. This strategy is also effective for the mother in getting away from difficult situations. If she hears something terrible that she doesn't want to deal with, feigning a particular illness is her next option. If you listened to this phrase, "Don't break the news to your mother, or her sickness would worsen," then you may have been dealing with a Psychosomatic mother.

In addition to caring for her, another way to get attention from this mother is to fall sick too. This is something many children find out later on. The reason for this is that being sick makes them connect on mutual ground. However, if the sickness of the child is worse than that of the mother, and ends up taking up all of the attention, the mother will not be pleased with it. She feels entitled to all the care and won't be happy when her child takes it all.

For example, Mark's mother was always sick, and most times, he came running home whenever she called. Soon, his dad had a stroke, and he began to spend most of his time caring for his dad. However, he soon realized that his mother continued to come up with something worse to get attention. Her goal was to be sicker than her husband so she could get more attention from Mark.

At some point, she claimed to be in an accident, and Mark rushed home only to realize nothing of that sort happened. Of course, he soon got tired of her antics and refused to show up the next time she called. This resulted in a barrage of nasty emails and calls claiming that Mark never loved her or cared for her.

The flamboyant, extroverted mother

This one is the ideal mother for everyone out there. She is loved by everyone, neighbors, friends, and even random strangers because she is adorable and friendly. She has it all going in the public eye, and she continually strives to maintain that image. She will be offended by anyone or anything that might seem to change this perception. However, she secretly is a monster in her home to the children. She will control them and be mean to them, but still ensuring that whatever they do in the public eye always makes her look like the best mother in the world. The children fear her and cannot seek any form of help as they feel like there is no way out, and no one would believe them anyway.

The Addicted Narcissistic mother

These narcissistic mothers deal with substance abuse. However, their behavior is more prominent whenever they are under the influence of any substance they are addicted to. Anytime the effect of the substance wears off, they portray fewer narcissistic behaviors. But sometimes this is not the case.

To these mothers, their priority the substance they have a problem with. Nobody else matters until they satisfy their addiction. They must cater to their addiction before they do anything else.

For example, Liz's mother loved to attend parties. Most times, she left Liz to care for herself while her mother went out for those long night parties. She always came home stoned or drunk and went directly to sleep. This quickly became embarrassing for Liz, who called her mother out on this behavior. Her mother responded by saying, "Caring for you is hard work; I deserve some time to have fun!" This is followed by numerous comments that make Liz feel guilty for trying to complain. If her mother has to choose between her parties and the needs of her daughter, she chooses her parties..

The Subtly Abusive

These mothers share some similarities with extrovert mothers. They are very particular about how those on the outside see them and would prefer if no one outside was aware of her abuses at home. These mothers usually have a personality they display in private and a different one in public.

On the outside, they are the kindest, sweetest, loving, and most sensitive mother, any child, can have. However, when they are home, they become mean and abusive. For children who live with these types of mothers, their lives can be a confusing one. The same behavior her child portrays outside which the mother welcomes with a smile, will probably be met with an angry response when in the confines of the home.

Also, this mother can say one thing in public and say something entirely different in private. For instance, when in public, she could announce to everyone in a room how proud she is of her child. But in private, she will continuously tell her child how much of a disappointment they are. This kind of inconsistent behavior can be very confusing for the child and can lead to a long-term ripple effect.

For example, Natasha's mother was loving and could never hurt a fly in public. But in the home, it was an entirely different situation. At home, she gave priority to her feelings over those of everyone else's, including Natasha's. If Natasha needed a shoulder to lean on at home, her mother was quick to dismiss her when she went to her mother for help. But in public, her mother was loving and caring. All of their problems were limited to the confines of the home.

The Smothering Mother

The Smothering Mother believes that the world is all about her like any good narcissist would. So, what's the catch? Why would they look outside of themselves to "smother" you with attention? Well, the key thing here is that the Smothering Mother considers you as an extension of her — in a not healthy way. You may think of yourself as your person, but to your narcissistic Smothering Mother, you are them.

This kind of narcissistic mother is all about running your life, whether or not you agree with her verdict on things. She'll try to tell you who to date and not date, how to act, what to wear and not wear, whether or not you should take that trip to the Bahamas with your husband.

Speaking of husbands, your Smothering Mother has no sense of boundaries. Nothing is off the table for her. She will go so far as to inquire about how things are in the bedroom between you and your significant other — and she won't think much of it. If you refuse to share those details with her, then you're a monster for not answering such perfectly "reasonable" questions about your sex life. The Smothering Mother also doesn't have a problem sharing details about her sex-escapades, if it means it gets you to talk. It doesn't matter how young you are. She's ready to have those conversations with you, anytime.

The "Smother" will project all her desires onto you. She'll insist that you love amusement parks when you don't. She is the one who does, but remembers, you're an extension of her! Whatever is the case for her is the case for you. No questions asked.

The Smother will also insert herself into your children's lives. She'll tell you you're not raising them right and will try to take over from you. You'll set rules and boundaries for your kids, and your Smother will undermine them and walk all over your authority. She'll even push a step further to make your kids begin to disregard you and prefer their Grand Smother instead. The Smother is the one who frequently tells your kids, "Never mind your mother. She doesn't know what she's talking about." The result is that this winds up being weird for your kids. They're confused as to whose authority they should defer to. This abuse can go on and on for generations if you let the Smother have her way.

What better way for the Smother to control you than to be near you! Now, do not get me wrong. There are amazing relationships between mothers and their daughters. This is not the case. It only seems that way, until you look a little closer.

It's incredibly challenging to get away from the Smother because it never even occurs to you that they've got you caged and doing tricks on their command. Even when you do realize it, it's a bit hard for you to cut loose because of all the years of conditioning you've gone through, among other things.

The Emotionally Needy

Most narcissistic mothers have this trait. However, those mothers in this category make it more prominent than others. They dump all of their emotional baggage on their children and expect them to listen, care for, and understand her. In time, the children begin to play the roles of therapists trying to solve problems they should not have any business solving in the first place. While this is going on, the emotional needs of the children are ignored, and even when they do garner the courage to ask their mother for help, the help they get from her is almost insignificant. If it is not about her, then it is not essential.

For example, Diane had a rough day at work. First, she lost her wallet, and her vehicle was repossessed because she was unable to continue her payments. After walking home under the rain, she arrives home and tries to speak to her mother about how her day was. Instead of listening, her mother says something in the lines of, "My day was much worse! Yours is nothing."

Then she goes ahead to tell Diane about her day instead. Over time, Diane has grown to understand that her mother's stories are always unbeatable, so she lets it go and listens to her mother. She bottles up her feelings in the process, knowing that she would never get any help from her mother.

The mean mother

This one is mean to her children and will not want her children to have what she cannot have or never had. She will continuously interfere in the good things that the children might have, so she can always be the one looking good or being praised. She will not let the daughter have a good car if she doesn't have one. She will not let the son have a beautiful house if she has not built one for her. This limits her children so much, as they cannot make any progress in life that is better than hers. The children end up doing things in secret so they can enjoy some luxuries without her knowledge.

The success-oriented mother

This one is only concerned about what the children accomplish and nothing else. She will continuously compare her children with their peers if they do look like they have more accomplishments than her children. She is continuously happy when her children get easy things, especially if she knows she can benefit from them. She is delighted to visit her children in big homes, be driven around in big cars, and boast of how successful her family is. Anyone that is not successful in her family will continuously be intimidated and ignored, as she will always make it clear that she does not associate with failures. These kinds of mothers push their children too hard that they cannot think of anything else except the next best car, phone, etc.

The Blanking Mother

For the Blanking Mother, you simply do not exist. You're a blank. She looks at you, but not quite because, for her, there's nothing there. You don't exist. She's not going to bother taking care of you. She will neglect you and all your needs. She won't bother to teach you the basics of life and living. She won't bother with your achievements in school. She won't show for PTA. She never praises you for anything, and if she does, it's backhanded at best. But she will go on and on about the achievements of the other kids, and how it's sad that you could never do much better than them.

The sad thing about growing up with a Blanking Mother is you might find yourself continually needing to draw attention to yourself — not necessarily because you seek to be admired, or worshipped or any of that crap, but because you need to know that you exist. You need to know you are seen.

Notes:

_____
_____
_____
_____
_____
_____
_____
_____
_____
_____
_____
_____
_____
_____
_____
_____
_____
_____
_____
_____
_____
_____
_____
_____
_____
_____
_____

Narcissistic Mothers

Chapter 3: How your Mother will manifest her Narcissism

This behavior can be hard to recognize because such mothers make it look like it is typical for how they go about treating their family. However, there are obvious and repetitive behaviors she will have that will ultimately stand out to make one know they are dealing with a narcissistic mother:

She is two-faced

Such mothers will portray very different personalities in social settings and at home. They are very happy and perfect in other people's eyes, but become controlling and very insecure at home. She will praise her children and adore them in public, only to demean, criticize, and bring them down when they are behind closed doors. This always comes as a surprise to the children as they would not know how to behave or relate with the mother. They will be cautious with her and work their best to please her in public, which only creates multiple personalities for the whole family.

Claims your success

A narcissist mother will always request her children's progress. Anything that they do well or succeed in, she will say it is because of them that you have achieved greatness. And they will make you grateful that they are your mother because through that, you have become successful. That way, anytime you make a great achievement, you will automatically feel like you owe it to her and that it is a favor to you. It becomes more stressful for the child because you are forced to out-perform yourself just to make her happy.

She is easily offended

One slight mistake or move and she hits the roof with anger. She would also constantly make it seem like she does so much for the child, but the child is very ungrateful. She also gets easily angered when her demands are not met immediately. She would use words like "I took you to school for nothing" or "You love your wife more than me, your mother." This pushes the child to the edge, and they always end up falling for her demands to avoid conflict.

Makes you feel nervous

Since her constant downplaying of her children makes them lose their confidence, they automatically think nervous whenever she is around. This is because she is unpredictable to every little situation and reacts on impulse. The children get scared even when they have done something great, as they do not know what her reaction will ultimately be. They know she can never praise them for any good deed unless it benefits her. This leaves them always on edge with her around, as she ensures she has instigated self-doubt in the children such that they can never believe in their capabilities.

Finds fault in everything

They just can never appreciate the effort or validate any good deed. They will always see a better way of doing something, which would have been easier or faster according to her opinion. This means she can never take apologies, as she also wants perfection, which the family can never achieve. She will continuously demean the efforts made by anyone, always saying someone else or herself would have done it better.

Everything revolves around her

The world revolves around her, and everything everyone does is targeted at her. She takes everything personally, even when no ill intent was involved. If anything happens without her consent or knowledge, she would be mad and feel left out. She also wants to be informed on every move the children make, so she can ensure she has controlled the outcome to her liking.

Makes you feel like a failure

She will make you feel bad about your own decisions that are not what she may want at that time. She will make comments like so and so would have done better, or tell you that you are not doing well enough. She might even say she is not meant to raise failures. This mostly comes about when the child has not fulfilled her needs or got her what she wants.

Competes with her children

The mother will tend to be in constant competition with her children, doing what they do or insinuating that she can do better than them. She can also always make them feel like she is better at things at her old age compared to them, who are young. This can be in matters of beauty or evens sexual prowess.

She has a sense of entitlement and superiority

When the narcissist looks at the world, they see that it is in black and white. With the narcissist, there is a hierarchy in the world, and narcissist likes to put themselves at the top. This is the only place where the narcissist is going to feel like they are safe. The narcissists, at least in their minds, have to be the best, the most competent, and the most right.

She has a vast need for validation and attention

Narcissists are always going to need a lot of attention. They need it constantly. These are the people who will follow their victim around the house, asking the other person to find things for them (even though they are perfectly capable of doing it on their own), and saying anything that is going to grab your attention. Even then, this doesn't seem to be enough for the narcissist.

She needs to be in control

Since narcissists are always going to be disappointed in the way that life unfolds around them, they are going to do what they can to try and control it, to see if they can mold it in some way to their liking. In the mind of the narcissist, there is going to be a storyline about what each character, in a specific interaction, should be doing and saying. Of course, the real world doesn't follow this storyline, and when that happens, the narcissist is going to feel upset about it. They will get mad and try to control the situation to their liking.

She like to blame and deflect

Even though the narcissist is going to insist that they are the ones who are in control, they are never going to be responsible for any adverse results. If the results of their power are good, they will jump right in and expect all of the praise and adoration that they think they deserve. However, if things don't fall into place or things don't go according to the plan that they had, then the narcissist will refuse to take the blame.

She has trouble communicating at work or inability to work as part of a team

They do not understand how others feel, and they have no want to learn how to do this either. So they are less likely to get along. They won't give in, they won't admit when they are wrong, but they will undoubtedly take all of the credit when things start going well. They are tough to work with and can make the whole team feel frustrated.

As you can see, a lot of the traits that come with being a narcissist are going to make it difficult for them to get along in society and do well. They are not able to understand the way that ordinary people are going to think, and they are much more interested in making sure that they are the ones who are in charge, and that the ones that get what they need. This can make it a challenge for them to get along well with others.

She is Inflexible

Narcissistic mothers tend to be rigid in their decisions about their kids. They will regulate the kids to the minor details, and try to make sure the kids live up to their billing. If the kid transgresses even by a small part, they will be very nasty and upset.

They are also irritable and touchy, and the main reason for being touchy is that they aren't getting the kind of attention they expected from the onset. They also see their kids be having a lot of faults and shortcomings.

She has Zero Empathy

The narcissistic mother doesn't have any feelings towards the child. They don't put the thoughts and feelings of the child in perspective. If they have time to recognize the feelings and thoughts, they will fail to validate them to be vital to the process. At this time, only what the mother feels and thinks is important.

Children that are faced with this type of influence might respond in various ways – they might decide to fight back so that they stand up for themselves, they might decide to distance themselves from the parents or decider to freeze the parent out and come up with a false persona. The latter usually leads to narcissistic traits.

They don't have the time to understand what other people are feeling at all times. They also rarely apologize or feel guilty.

She is Possessive

Here, the narcissistic mother expects the kid to dwell fully under her influence the whole time. When the kid starts to become mature and independent, the mother will not like it and will become extremely jealous.

Any time the kid tries to leave the fold, the mother doesn't want to hear about it. For instance, when the kid makes new friends, the mother will always find a reason to push them away.

She Neglect

In many situations, narcissistic mothers will choose to focus on their interests, and they neglect their kids in the process. The activities give the narcissist the self-importance and validation that she always craves. This includes hobbies, career progression, and much more. The mother then leaves the child to the other parent or on their own.

She Projects Her Desires Through You

Narcissists only can care for themselves and no one else. This is the case even with narcissistic parents. They tend to live through the lives of their children in really unhealthy ways. For instance, if a parent had experiences she desired when she was younger but was unable to achieve it, she may try to live it through her kids.

She is Never Wrong

As humans, it is reasonable to have disagreements and arguments. During these arguments, you will learn that sometimes you were wrong, and other times you were right. No one is always right, and this is the same case for everyone.

However, narcissists believe they are always right and never at fault. This is the case, especially when it involves a narcissistic mother. She makes herself the victim anytime there is an argument, even when the argument does not concern her.

During arguments, instead of accepting her faults and making amends, she becomes defensive and may even try to guilt-trip you.

Your Needs Does Not Matter to her

Narcissists give themselves priority above anyone else. Narcissistic parents often ignore their kids and pay attention to their own needs above. Narcissistic mothers, instead of caring for her children, may focus on her hobbies, career, and other things she believes are more important.

Due to this, children of narcissistic parents often learn to fend for themselves at an early age. If the majority of your childhood was spent with family members, nannies, by yourself, or with other guardians, then you may have had a narcissistic mother.

It is Easy to Offend Her

Narcissists always crave attention. In fact, they thrive on this attention and would do all they can to get it. Parents in this category look for any reason to be offended, especially when they feel they are being criticized. Even the most straightforward and irrelevant things can get a narcissistic parent offended.

She Places All Her Emotional Burden On You

This is very common in homes with single parents. Under normal circumstances, having a proper line of communication between both parents and kids is not a bad thing, but when you have started to play the role of a therapist to your mother, then it is a huge problem.

Ideally, parents should be responsible for meeting the emotional needs of their kids. They are the ones children should be able to run to when there is a problem and get help. However, when the roles become reversed and stay this way, then this could be a sign of trouble.

She Diverts All Conversations to Herself

By now, you should understand that attention is something narcissists can't do without. Narcissistic parents like to make every conversation about them. For instance, if you are having a conversation about something important that happened to you, narcissistic mothers always find a way to make it about them. Rather than listening to you, they ignore what you are saying and instead make it about them.

She Is Extremely Competitive

In healthy relationships between parents and kids, the parents may sometimes allow their kids to beat them at games. These could be when playing board games, video games, or races. The reason for doing this is to encourage a healthy spirit of competition. It also helps build confidence in kids. This is also the case with a few animals that let the younger ones win.

She doesn't care about how she achieves this, even if she has to go through some plastic surgery. Sometimes she may even flirt around during gatherings to ensure attention does not deviate from her. Competition can also come in other areas like finance, sports, and so on.

She Puts You Down

A narcissistic mother will leverage insults, criticism, and manipulation to reduce the confidence of their kids. Sometimes, she may downplay their achievements even though her children have done well. The only time your results are acknowledged is when she can take full credit for it.

She enjoys destroying the joy that comes from achieving a feat, and she goes all out to achieve this. Regardless of what you do, she can't help but put you down for it to make herself feel good. If you deal with all of these, then it is an indication that you have a narcissistic mother.

She Hold Grudges

Narcissistic mothers hold grudges against those who they feel have offended them, including their kids. They can carry these grudges for extremely long periods, even for something as little as doing something they did not support. Their way of handling this would be to ignore the kids completely for stuff that healthy people would have long forgotten.

She Uses Love and Affection as Weapons

Narcissistic mothers understand how important love and affection are to their kids, and they use it to their advantage. As a form of reward, they show love and friendship to their kids when they do things they want. And when they do show this love, they ensure it is in the full glare of the public, so they are deemed, good parents.

She Does Not Respect Boundaries

Narcissistic mothers don't respect the boundaries of their kids. They may take up their time and even the properties of their kids without permission. There is no privacy in your bedroom either as she can waltz in at any moment without warning. When this happens, the only reason you get is that it is her home, and she can do whatever she wants. Even as an adult, she may barge into your household without notice or regard for your privacy.

She is Childish

Narcissistic mothers are petty and childish. When you refuse to fall for her antics, she throws tantrums and cries that you have no love for her. If you do something she does not agree with, she will continuously whine and nag about it in a bid to guilt-trip you.

She is Irresponsible

Many times, the narcissist will blame one person that they are firmly attached to, such as the husband or the wife. This is all aimed at maintaining that façade of perfection that they have to manage. They do this because they understand that you are the only person they can blame without having to lose.

She is Motivated by Fear

The whole life of a narcissistic mother is motivated by fear. They feed on fear and get energized when someone is afraid due to their actions. Most of the mothers' have concerns that are repressed and deeply buried. They have a constant fear of being on the wrong, rejected, and ridiculed.

She is Always Anxious

Anxiety is a vague feeling that something terrible will happen. Many people that suffer from NPD have this anxiety that something terrible will happen. While many might show this openly, others don't do it, and they keep the feelings repressed.

Notes:

_____

_____

_____

_____

_____

_____

_____

_____

_____

_____

_____

_____

_____

_____

_____

_____

_____

_____

_____

_____

_____

_____

_____

_____

_____

_____

_____

Narcissistic Mothers

Chapter 4 : Narcissist Mothers and Their Daughters

Narcissistic mothers affect their daughters differently from their sons. For many daughters, the significant impact of the mother-daughter relationship is that it gives her an unhealthy style of attachment, which becomes evident in her connections in the future. For some, it could be an issue in trusting people or difficulties in saying how they feel.

The effects of being raised by narcissistic mothers last for the better part of a daughter's life. If she is a golden child, her self-esteem may be non-existent because she will only be a vessel for projecting her mother's desires. This is the case with many golden children. She may further become a narcissist herself as the best way of dealing with the world at large.

On the other hand, the scapegoat daughter, after dealing with years of abuse, may stay away from confrontations, and never say the things she is feeling. This may spread further in her life as an adult, leaving her entirely without a voice.

Narcissistic mother's daughters grow up under a threatening female shadow. The two major characteristics of this exploitative upbringing are the lack of empathy and complete control. A narcissistic mother is actively trying to make her duplicate in her daughter, which means she is projecting her insecurities and ego into her. The care is characterized by suffering, dependence, and self-denial. However, they never get a solution for this and always end up concluding that their moms had no maternal instincts. Narcissism is complicated and harmful and will try to erase and squash any attempts for independence by their daughters.

Growing under narcissistic mothers can be tricky. Mothers tend to project themselves into their daughters, making them a blank canvas for their ego. However, they still perceive their daughters as a threat and think that if they get a chance, they can surpass them. It doesn't matter in what terms, whether independence, resolve, intelligence, or even beauty. Their daughters, therefore, find it exhausting and complicated to maintain a relationship with their narcissistic mother. They miss out on motherly empathy from their own mothers. More often, the narcissistic mother establishes unmerciful discipline for their daughters. They are more considerate of how the world sees their daughter rather than understanding what she needs, what she wants, or how she feels. As a result, they erase their daughter's emotions through criticism or indifference. They grow with helpless, low self-confidence, and self-esteem and will seek their mother's approval whenever they have to make a decision.

Narcissistic mothers create love triangles between them and their daughters and bring in other people's opinions to justify their point of view. They do this to purposely play with the emotions of their daughters and have total control over them. Triangulation entails bringing another person in the dynamic of the relationship, whether a complete stranger, a relative, a current mistress, or an ex-lover. A narcissistic mother can use triangulation in person, social media, or through her own verbal accounts of the daughter. She will always rely on jealousy as an effective emotion, which will cause the daughter to compete for her affections. She will use provocative phrases like "I wish he would come back in my life" or "I wish you were like her."

Ways the daughter of narcissistic mothers can be affected:

She is Not Emotionally Developed

Throughout their lives growing up, the daughters of narcissistic mothers try to live to satisfy her as opposed to living a life they truly desire. One primary reason for doing this is to win the love and affection of her mother, which, as we know by now, may never come. During the process of doing this, the daughter tends to let go of or deny her own emotions, making her forget who she is.

Her Self-Esteem is Not Genuine

After growing up through childhood with unrealistic compliments and love from her narcissistic mother, which she uses to validate herself, she builds self-esteem based on that.

This is not real love, and neither are the complements real, but the daughter of the narcissist fails to notice even into adulthood. As adults, they then seek relationships with people who would make her feel as good as her mother did but would hardly find a comparable relationship, leading to a vicious and never-ending cycle.

She is Not Happy and Does Not Understand Why

As kids, we tend to categorize all of the things we experience in the home as normal. Many children even make the mistake of believing that this is how it plays in every typical home. For the daughter of the narcissistic mother, this is especially the case because she is always struggling to be her mother's golden child, to get her attention and love. Even if she is successful in getting these from her mother, she finds out that she is not happy. This is because what she is spending all her effort and time trying to get is not genuine love.

Intimacy Scares Her

The daughter of the narcissist is not comfortable with genuinely becoming intimate with anyone. This is because it is not something that she has grown accustomed to in her life. Because she believes love is a form of transaction that you pay for in some manner, she may never truly love anyone and will think there are conditions attached.

She is Sensitive to Rejection

The daughter of a narcissistic mother grows to understand that at one point, they can be the golden child. She also knows that she can quickly become the scapegoat as well if she doesn't make her mother happy. As a result of this, the daughters grow into adults with this mindset, always trying to please those they date and their friends. However, she will always be on the lookout for possible rejection and trouble.

She is Drawn to Partners with Narcissistic Behaviors

Daughters who have lived with abuse from their narcissistic mothers their entire lives become used to this feeling. They grow into adults seeing this as normal and find themselves being drawn to those who have similar characteristics as their mother, who would similarly treat them.

Fear of Failure

Growing up, daughters of narcissistic mothers learn that they need to be perfect. This is particularly the case for the golden child. She understands that she can easily experience the wrath of her mother if she fails to meet the desired expectations. For this reason, many daughters from narcissistic families do not leave their comfort zones because they are afraid to fail. Others who do leave their comfort zones and try to achieve something worth celebrating, never really take credit for this achievement. This is because they have grown accustomed to their mothers taking credit for any of their accomplishments.

There Will Always Be Scapegoats and Special Ones

The daughters who are raised in homes run by narcissistic mothers grow up believing that the world is divided into categories. One category consisting of special ones and the other with scapegoats.

This is the way the narcissistic mother runs the home, and the daughter takes the lessons she learned into the real world. It also spreads down to her relationships as she feels you are either on the right team or a scapegoat.

She Feels Manipulation and Verbal Abuse Are Normal

As the daughter grows older, she is unable to determine what is healthy and what is abuse. She begins to categorize these sorts of behaviors as usual and would expect them in every relationship she enters even as an adult. This is why many daughters of narcissistic mothers tend to find someone who similarly treats them.

How a narcissistic mother treats her daughter?

A narcissistic mother exhibits a neglectful, non-validating, and non-nurturing parental style. Their style is extremely dysfunctional and completely interferes with the natural development of her daughter. Functional parents easily accept the natural traits in their children and will assist them at every stage of their maturation phase. For instance, every child will need to feel immature (the ability of being childish at some stage), dependent, (ability to rely on the caregiver on her emotional and physical needs), imperfect (ability to make mistakes without feeling toxic-shame), vulnerable (the ability to picture oneself passionately through scholarly attainment of exhibited parental limits), and valuable (able to esteem oneself in the middle of others). However, for a dysfunctional narcissistic-led family, some aspects like self-centered and childish behaviors are strongly prohibited. Following the narcissistic mother's belief, such behaviors will interfere with their obsessive desires of having their needs met and being at the center of the attention. If, by any means, the daughter tries to behave naturally, for instance, being immature, dependent, imperfect, or vulnerable, then the mother will always confront her with questions such as "Is there something wrong with you? Style up." After some subsequent warnings, the message is eventually strengthened, forcing the kid to expense her feelings and needs for her mother.

She always subjects her daughter to toxic shame

A daughter raised by a narcissistic mother rarely feels accepted for being herself. She is faced with the dilemma of choosing between her mother's love and sacrificing herself, and as a result, a pattern of self-denial and accommodation is repeated as codependency in her adult relationships.

She ensures that her daughter is emotionally unavailable

For a daughter of a narcissistic mother, the closeness and comfort provided naturally by the maternal caring and tenderness are absent. The narcissistic mother might offer her daughter with all the necessary physical needs, but she will leave her emotionally bereft. Sadly, the daughter never realizes what is missing, and she continually seeks warmth and understanding from her mother that she witnesses or experiences with her friends or relatives in other mother-daughter relationships.

She is always in Control

A narcissistic mother is still blind. She set things up and ensures that their world revolves around them. They abusively manipulate and control their daughter's choices, feelings, and needs whenever they can. Based on the concept of self-involvement, the narcissistic mother will tend to neglect and deprive their daughter while they focus on themselves and their sons. They consider their daughters as an extension of themselves and thus live through them.

She is always in competition with her daughter

Since a narcissistic mother believes that she is the best of all, she creates a stiff competition with her daughter for the husband's or son's love. She refuses to protect her daughter if, by any chance, she abuses her. She goes to extremes and even disparages or restricts her daughter's boyfriends because, according to her, they are not good enough, but she would still compete with them to seek for her daughter's attention. Additionally, she invades the private life of her daughter. She undermines the existing relationships with relatives or friends just to make sure she is in control and the number one priority in her daughter's life.

Notes:

_____
_____
_____
_____
_____
_____
_____
_____
_____
_____
_____
_____
_____
_____
_____
_____
_____
_____
_____
_____
_____
_____
_____
_____
_____
_____
_____
_____
_____

Narcissistic Mothers

Chapter 5: Narcissist Mothers and their Sons

There are many ways the sons of narcissistic mothers are treated. Below, we will be looking at a few of these ways using their categories.

The Golden Child

Sons who are assigned the role of a golden child tend to become full-blown narcissists later on because of how they are raised.

They always believe they deserve better than all of the other average individuals in the world. The following are some of the different ways the mother of the narcissist affects the son in this category.

He is What His Mother Projects

The golden child may never find out that everything he did was what his mother projected onto him. They may also never stop trying to satisfy their mothers all through their lives. Because he spends most of his time being the vessel that his mother projects onto him, he may never become the man he was meant to be, but instead becomes the one his mother wishes he was.

His mother will continuously let him know how handsome and perfect he is. But this does not mean he is also free from emotional abuse from his mother too. Since she always wants him to be dependent on her, she may switch between boosting his confidence and little forms of manipulation here and there.

He Continuously Caters to His Mother's Needs

Other times, the mother shows excessive affection to her son in a manner that may not be appropriate. However, to the golden child who only knows what his mother teaches him, there is nothing wrong with this behavior. He learns to cater to the desire of his mother, especially if he hopes to get love and affection from her.

Sometimes, sons in this category grow into men that are easily abused.

There Are Problems in His Relationships

The sons of the narcissistic mother may find it challenging to grow proper relationships. This is because they are forever trying to please their mother and remain under her control. Also, when they do find someone their heart desires and want to date, their mothers will never agree. This is because she feels no woman is perfect for her son, and every woman wants to steal the mother's property (her son) from her. In most cases, she does all she can to frustrate these women until they leave. Those who choose to stay suffer constant criticism and abuse in the hopes that they eventually leave.

He Experiences Emotional Instability

These sons never have stable emotions. For many of them, there is bottled-up anger because even though they do everything to please their mother, they do not like the fact that she destroys their relationships and lives. Nonetheless, they are unable to tell their mothers how they feel and channel their anger to other women.

They Have Difficulty in Breaking Free

For the golden sons who decide to break free and get independence from their mothers, the scenario is different. Their mothers find their idea of independence as rebellion. Due to this, the mothers do everything possible to punish them by seeking vengeance.

The Scapegoat Son

Unlike the golden son, who has lived the happiest life, the scapegoat son is the opposite. Because they get the blame for everything that goes wrong in the home, they grow to blame themselves for everything, even things that they are not responsible for.

The following are a few ways the scapegoat son reacts to his mother's treatment:

He Always Tries to Please His Mother

The scapegoat son will do everything possible to get recognition from his mother, or at least leave the scapegoat role. However, the treatment they get won't change. Sometimes, she may show him a little affection to keep him going, but the behavior will stay the same.

His mother insults him constantly, from his achievements down to his looks. Even though this son does not enjoy the treatment he gets from his mother, he is desperate for her love, and that keeps him going back.

He Adopts Bad Behaviors

Some sons in this category react to all of the insults and treatment their mother dishes out to them by becoming truants. Some of them lash out in their community or school. Others leave home and never return and may begin to hang around other kids with similar problems. The constant insults and nagging about how they are failures start to take effect in their lives, and as a result, some of them may have problems with substances.

As adults, even regular failures, everyone deals with serves as a reinforcement for everything their mother told them when they were younger. Many of them make no effort to correct this notion once they have failed a few times..

He Has Problems with Relationships

When a scapegoat son gets into a relationship, the insults they get from their mothers do not stop. The mother may even dish out these insults in the presence of partners or prospective partners in a bid to make the scapegoat less appealing to them. To do this, she may leverage the son's weaknesses and expose them to the prospect. Even if the relationships do survive, the possibility of it being a success is not high as these sons don't know how to deal with a healthy relationship.

The Forgotten Sons

These sons may not have as many problems as the other categories. This is because they grew up being ignored. They don't get any bad nor good attention from their mother, and this includes manipulation and abuse.

At an early age, these sons learn to fend for themselves and learn to grow up fast. Sometimes they may leave home and find better families who will show them genuine love, but this is not always the case.

Regardless of whether these sons are rejected or ignored, they always feel a sense of abandonment. They still harbor the feeling that they may have done some irreparable harm that can't be forgiven, which is why everyone neglects them. He will always feel responsible for his mother, rejecting him even in his adult life.

For many, a way of dealing with this pain is to capitalize on alcohol and other substances that may work for a while before further worsening their situation.

Regardless of the roles, children from narcissistic homes are assigned to, and the effects can be damaging and last for their entire lives. Narcissistic mothers are controlling and would take their son's achievements as theirs. Those they are unable to take credit for will be deemed insignificant, and if their sons fail, they get insulted and abused.

These mothers only put in the effort when it can make them seem better than they are. Since the narcissistic mother is worried about her image, she does everything to make sure it is seen as perfect.

Your mother hurt you, and it is understandable that you are angry and hurt for everything she did to you. All of the abuse you may have encountered may be difficult to deal with.

Don't dwell on the shame and guilt because all of these were circumstances beyond your control. However, at this point, you need to heal, so you need to give yourself that chance. Healing will require a ton of patience, commitment, effort, and time.

Notes:

_____
_____
_____
_____
_____
_____
_____
_____
_____
_____
_____
_____
_____
_____
_____
_____
_____
_____
_____
_____
_____
_____
_____
_____
_____
_____
_____
_____
_____

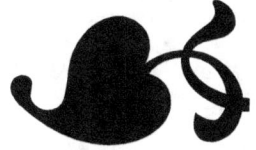

Chapter 6: Narcissistic mother-in-Law

Narcissistic Mothers-in-law are complicated creatures. They are often misunderstood, and in reality, not many daughters-in-law or sons-in-law take the time to get to know them and understand them entirely and where they're coming from. Is getting along with your mother-in-law impossible then? Or is there something you can do on your part to facilitate a better relationship with the woman who bore and raised your spouse?

Do you have a difficult mother-in-law? Are you just about ready to give up on trying to have a civil relationship with her? This chapter is going to provide you with specific solutions for coping with a controlling, intrusive, and inconsiderate mother-in-law. Learn how to get along with her sooner rather than later, so that you can avoid inadvertently hurting your spouse and children and meanwhile enjoy your married life in peace.

Sadly, many couples enter a marriage with a pre-made decision that their mother-in-law is going to be a problem. It may sound surprising, but your mother-in-law does not have to be a problem at all. Before making up your mind that she is an ogre, at least give her a chance. Instead of starting your marriage wary and ready to hate her, make it your goal to have a good relationship with her. Start your marriage with this particular objective in mind and not by automatically hating her. Forget what the media dictates you ought to feel about your mother-in-law.

Why is your mother-in-law always dropping by your home unannounced? Why does she call you on your cell phone ten times a day? What could have driven her to pick up your kids and take them shopping? Give her the benefit of the doubt. In reality, many mothers-in-law are just misunderstood older women. And while it is easier for some to conclude that they are terrible persons, isn't there a chance that she's only a lonely mother who misses her child and wants to be more involved in her grandchildren's lives?

And even when your mother-in-law is absolutely the worst, still try to make some sense of why she acts that way. Asking your spouse to shed some light on this will help you get a better perspective of things. Does your significant other agree with your perception of his or her mother? If you can relate to her life and experiences, perhaps, you may be able to interact with her better.

Let's just accept the fact that some mothers-in-law are difficult to deal with. These mothers-in-law are overbearing, inconsiderate, controlling, and manipulative. So does it mean that you have to live a miserable existence? Will you then give her victory by ending your marriage? Before you make any crazy decisions, you need to know that you can still keep your marriage and make it a happy one. Here's what you can do:

Drop Your Weapons

There is no need to be always so defensive when dealing with your mother-in-law. In general, people can sense when others are being defensive or guarded, and as a result, they, too, will raise their defenses. When a wall is created between two parties, effective communication and the development of a real and meaningful relationship becomes impossible. When you meet with your mother-in-law, lay down your weapon. Put down your defenses because this person is not your enemy. There is no need for you to take a fight stance. Instead of considering your mother-in-law an adversary, think of her as a useful ally. By doing so, you can change how you see her and will be able to treat her warmly.

Setting Healthy Boundaries

Setting boundaries for every relationship is part of maintaining healthy self-esteem.

To set boundaries, ask yourself what is acceptable to you and what is not. You must be able to clearly define the limitations you want to set in your relationship with your mother-in-law. Remember that the purpose of setting boundaries is to have a civil relationship with her and not to cut her off from her child and her grandchildren. As a guide, when setting your boundaries, always consider how involved you would like your mother-in-law to be in your married life.

Once you can define the boundaries for your mother-in-law, the next thing to do is to let her know about them. This part is always tricky because it could set off unpleasant drama and also lead to conflict. Nevertheless, you need to learn how to communicate with your mother-in-law effectively. At all times, remember to be polite and respectful, no matter how angry you are. Speak with tact and always be considerate of her feelings. Always take the high road and remember that being unpleasant, rude, or sarcastic will just escalate the conflict.

The best way to enforce your boundaries is to let her know that there are consequences when she fails to respect these. For example, when she drops by your home without calling first, remind her that you will appreciate it if she calls first and let you know that she would be visiting. The next time she comes to your house unannounced, tell her that you cannot entertain her at this time as you are busy with other chores. If she does it for the third time, it is now clear that she does not recognize your boundaries.

Maintain Emotional Detachment

Will you let your narcissistic mother-in-law ruin your day just because of some remark she made or the behavior she displayed? Think about it. The more power you give your mother-in-law over you and your marriage, the more formidable she becomes. So just stop letting her affect you. Tell yourself that she has no effect on you and that she will not generate a reaction from you. The more you detach yourself emotionally from your mother-in-law, the better your life will be. For instance, when she criticizes your hair and clothes, the kind of job you do, or the cleanliness of your home, just smile and say nothing. Most importantly, don't let her words affect you. Visualize that her words are drifting in the air and are gently being carried away by the wind, not entering your ear, heart, and mind, and having no effect on you whatsoever.

Stand Your Ground

Don't let yourself be bullied by the woman who is also the mother of your spouse. By this time, you may already be aware of how manipulative she can be, so be prepared for her tactics. Be ready for when she starts threatening you, using tears, or using your spouse to get you to do what she wants. She probably hates you anyway, so don't add to her reasons for doing so by being a coward. Stand your ground, especially for decisions concerning your marriage and your family.

Maintain your Distance

Distance is your friend. Especially during times when the narcissistic mother-in-law is just intolerable. One way to still get along with her and keep your sanity is to put some distance between you. If you can, move your family to another city or country, depending on your situation. But be warned because there are mothers-in-law that still cross thousands of miles just to barge in their child's home. If you live with your narcissistic mother-in-law, then save up and move out right away. If you don't live with her, then minimize your interaction with her. Show up for important family events, but remember that you don't need to attend all of it. And if you do see her, refrain from talking to her for a long time and avoid being alone in the room with her. The less time you spend with her, the less damage she can do to you.

Your mother-in-law is an essential person to your spouse and your children. Make sure you think about them every time you interact with your mother-in-law. Never be intentionally spiteful to her because you might end up hurting your spouse and your kids.

This woman will only become a threat if you allow her to be one. The best thing to do is to learn how to handle your relationship with her effectively. Also, always bear in mind that the link you have with your spouse is the most important. As long as you have a meaningful connection with your significant other, then your mother-in-law should not even be a cause of your concern.

If you have a difficult mother-in-law, you must never give her power over you. Yielding to a controlling and manipulative person throughout your marriage will eventually get to you, affecting the marriage that you so want to preserve. If you have a supportive spouse, then he or she can help you effectively deal with your mother-in-law so that you remain happy in your marriage. If your spouse is not willing to help you handle your issues with your mother-in-law or is not even willing to listen to your concerns, then this is another issue altogether, and you may want to start looking at your options.

Marriage is the union of two people who are in love. Although it is vital to value and respect the family your spouse came from, you did not say "I do" to the other's parents. A mother-in-law only becomes a problem when the couple gives her too much access in their lives. If the married couple is serious about creating an experience together, then both should learn to limit the involvement of their mothers, fathers, and siblings in their married life.

Notes:

_____

_____

_____

_____

_____

_____

_____

_____

_____

_____

_____

_____

_____

_____

_____

_____

_____

_____

_____

_____

_____

_____

_____

_____

_____

_____

_____

Narcissistic Mothers

Narcissistic Mothers

Chapter 7: A quick intro to NPD (Narcissistic Personality Disorder)

NPD can be categorized as a form of mental condition. It comes with various behavioral characteristics ranging from arrogance, lack of empathy, and many others. Narcissists tend to have this disorder, and this makes them manipulative, selfish, attention seekers.

NPD is a pathological mental disorder that often goes misdiagnosed by the medical community with the general public, also failing to recognize it as well.

The person that suffers from NPD doesn't have any empathy towards other people. Because of her self-regard, she doesn't recognize any actions that she makes can be unacceptable in society. She doesn't get ashamed at all, regardless of the situation.

This person fails to see that she isn't perfect, even when the situation that she is in forces her to admit her mistakes. Instead, she tries to justify her actions, the main reason why she is a thorn in the flesh of many.

Lack of emotional control usually comes as violent and silent mood swings that happen fast. At times, the narcissist can be fun and pleasant, but the next minute, she starts screaming, angry, and breaks things.

These people desire an insane amount of attention from others around them. You can notice these characteristics in people from various walks of life as narcissism is not limited to only a specific category of people. NPD has been known to have an impact on even the emotional behavior of these individuals.

Individuals with NPD symptoms love to be in control of things and fail to accept responsibility when they lose control. Instead of being accountable, they blame other individuals for it and are never at fault in any situation.

People who are battling with NPD always want to be ahead of others. They do this regardless of who gets hurt in the process. These individuals behave in this manner so that they can feel better about themselves. However, inside they are vulnerable and usually very unhappy. They are also enjoying abusing other individuals, and in comparison to the typical forms of abuse, this is subtle.

Educating yourself on everything that you can around narcissistic personality disorder, how it plays out in mother-daughter relationships, and how it has directly affected you as well as your symptoms can support you in understanding what you are experiencing. With this increased understanding, you can begin to identify where you are experiencing symptoms of this dysfunctional relationship in your life, why, and what can be done to help you heal them.

What Causes NPD?

The primary reason for NPD in people has not been ascertained. Nonetheless, there has been a range of theories brought up by behavioral experts as to why a person could develop this condition.

A few experts are of the school of thought that NPD is the result of numerous factors like the upbringing of the individual. If a child is made to feel less worthy at home consistently, he or she may feel alone. This may result in the child thinking there is no one else to turn to in the world, thereby living for only themselves and not minding the needs of others.

Children in this category grow up to actually believe they are better than everyone else, and their needs and desires should come first.

Other factors that can result in NPD while an individual is growing include trauma, continuous criticism, and abuse. Experts also believe that the sooner a person suffering from this condition is recognized, the less complicated it will be to get rid of the situation. If the individual can get treatment at the appropriate time, he or she can live a healthy life once more.

They are very sensitive and respond badly, and with violence even in the slightest disagreements, criticism, or perceived slights and often regard this as a personal attack. For instance, a narcissist would prefer to hold on to her demand to evade rages and indifference.

Notes:

Narcissistic Mothers

Chapter 8: Effect of Narcissistic Abuse On Adult Children

How a mother brings up a child determines a lot of how a child will turn out to be in the larger society. It hurts a child when a parent is a narcissist. The controlling and meanness always tend to make the children turn out into individuals that would have it rough fitting in the society. Below are some of the ways a narcissist mother hurts her children into adulthood:

Self-Doubt

The almost crippling self-doubt that you struggle with as an adult is caused by the contradiction between what your narcissistic mother told you, and what you could perceive with your senses. Add in the fact that your narcissistic mother continually says things to make you think you cannot trust your perception, and you can see how difficult it would be to be sure of yourself even as an adult.

Broken from Birth

When your mother is a narcissist, you get the feeling that you are deeply flawed. You feel like it's not even that you became faulty over time, but that you were born that way. You feel like you could never be fixed. You feel like there's something downright sick, evil, and wrong with you. You feel like you could never excise whatever parts of you that have all that twisted nastiness going on — mostly because it's not something you acquired, but inherently who you are.

Lack of Trust

As the child of a narcissistic mother, you find it incredibly hard to trust others. Not just any others, though. Women. In my case, it was any woman old enough to be my mother. I will not lie. I still struggle with this a bit. It's a challenge. It's like you expect every other woman to be just like your mother — unpredictable, manipulative, full of rage, toxic. Since growing up with a narc for a mom means you always had to be on your toes, this could then lead you to project your mother's traits onto others. You find yourself unable and unwilling to trust them. It also doesn't help that you keep finding yourself with narcissists for friends and lovers. The inclination is to keep your heart shut for good. Don't do that! There are good people, too.

Constantly Feeling Lonely

You might also find it incredibly difficult to establish connections with people outside of your family. Worst of all is the constant feeling like no matter where you go or who you're with, you never quite fit in. You don't feel like you belong anywhere at all.

Unrealistic Expectations of Yourself

Throughout your life with your narcissistic mother, she continued to feed you with a lie, through her actions, and words, covertly and overtly. What was the lie? That you could earn her love if you did your very best. So, you grew up thinking you just had to be smart enough, or pretty enough, or strong enough, or whatever-enough, and you would have the love, approval, and attention that your mother has been withholding from you. She made you believe that you had to strive to be a perfect child, and once you were perfect, then she could love you.

Staying in broken relationships

Most abused children will stay bad abusive relationships, as they do not know how to get out of it. They have been abused the whole of their lives; hence leaving is not an option. They tolerate it and keep enabling the abusers, as they would not know how to leave. They are also scared of what the other person in the relationship will feel, as they constantly put other people's feelings before theirs. This makes them stay in bad broken relationships, which only extends the abuse they have been going through as children into adulthood.

Post-traumatic stress disorders

Due to the long term trauma, most victims suffer from post-trauma stress. This extends into their day to day life where they will be scared to even get into relationships or may even develop anxiety attacks. Some will have to live off anti-depressants, as that will be the only way to cope. Some people have been hurt to the extent of committing suicide because of not knowing how their narcissistic mothers will handle some mistakes.

Seeking self-validation

While some children lose self-confidence, some start seeking the validation they never got from the people around them. They will always want to be praised and will not know it when they start turning into their abusive mothers. The unfortunate bit about this is their relationships with other people will always come to a dead-end because people will be overwhelmed by their demands and will not tolerate their behavior.

Lack of trust

An abused child will always have a hard time trusting anyone again with their feelings or emotions. This is because they will have been hurt and humiliated by the first person whom they trusted the most. It becomes even harder for them to trust a stranger, having been betrayed by the person closest to them. This will make them never fully commit to a long term relationship as they always expect the worst from people. They have to unlearn the mistrust first, so they can learn to trust again.

Being abusive

Some children pick the mantle from their mothers and carry the legacy on. Unfortunately, this will not be strange to them as they do not know better. They also start being abusive to their children as it is what they saw growing up. It becomes a cycle that can be very hard to break. One will have to make an intentional effort to work the effects of the abuse, and also accept the fact that they have a problem for them to get help and lead a different life from what their mother made them relate to.

You May Be Chronically Ashamed of Yourself

The shame that you experience now stems from always being made to feel inadequate as a child. Narcissistic mothers tend to be especially threatened by their daughters, which means that the level of abuse that you have experienced in terms of being put down and bullied is likely enormous. There is a good chance that your entire childhood was spent with you being told the many reasons as to why you were a bad person, and why you were not good enough. You were probably told that you were not deserving, not pretty, not smart, not worthy, and many other untrue things that were said to get you to stop bringing attention to yourself.

Childhood Abuse May Lead to Adulthood Abuse or Toxic Relationship Patterns

The reason why you may be experiencing toxic or abusive relationships now in adulthood is that you have never been taught boundaries or necessary self-care steps in life. Being raised by someone who commanded you to live your entire life based on her needs and desires has resulted in you not knowing how to fully stand up for yourself and take care of yourself in relationships now. This may be painful to admit, but, indeed, it is likely the reason why this is happening. If you notice that you seem to be surrounded by people who abuse you or take advantage of you and you cannot seem to understand why this happens, there is a good chance that it is a product of your groomed behaviors.

There May Be the Feeling of a Deep Void in Your Life

Even when you heal yourself from your mother's abuse, you are likely to find yourself in moments where you wish you had a healthy, supportive mother to rely on. You might even recall the times your mother showed you her charming mask, leading you to feel like maybe you can call her for support on just this one thing, hoping that she will offer that type of charm and support once again. It can be painful when you realize that your mother is unavailable to provide you with the support and the love that you need, and even more distressing when you know that she has no idea why you feel so disconnected and alone in the world due to her treatment.

They have impaired emotional intelligence

The daughter of a narcissistic mother detaches from her feelings and thoughts through her struggle to win her mother's emotions. This can be critical in a way that they will even have trouble identifying and naming their emotions, and as a result, they end up losing sight of themselves. When the daughter gets trapped in fulfilling the role of a good daughter, she is subjected to the extreme pressure of making her narcissistically defended her mother to feel and look good. She strives in both childhood and young adulthood to fulfill these needs through performance, achievement, and by maintaining good behavior. Her first priority is always making her mother look like a great mom, rather than her personal emotional growth and the independence of her needs. Upon growing up, the daughter takes the role of making her mum feel special, relevant, and needed. However, no matter the efforts she makes to ensure that her mom remains primary in her life, her narcissistic mother will still never recognize those.

They never develop real self-esteem and self-worth

For any child, self-worth is expected to build while he/she is still a child. When a child is well-taken care of and is shown real love, then this can be termed as a safe and perfect environment where the child can comfortably develop his/her self-esteem. However, when the child feels like her parent is never there for them, she will hardly build her self-esteem, and this seems like building a house out of soft clay rather than bricks.

They always have trust issues, and their ability to respond to threats is impaired

Living with a narcissistic mother can be very tricky. The mother expects constant fawning and making her feel good about herself. She becomes abusive and aggressive more frequently when the daughter fails to please her. She presents the abuse through emotional, mental, or physical torture, or the three of them altogether. In this family, the daughter is like always walking on eggshells, where she is more cautious not to piss her mother than doing what is right.

Difficulty parenting their own families with empathy

Children always learn to parent by observing their parents' parenting qualities. They find that whatever they were raised with feels natural and healthy. Daughters raised by a narcissistic mother will find it difficult to offer their children with lovely times like sitting and having a one-on-one conversation with them.

They turn out to be a complete doormat

To draw the attention she needs, a narcissistic mother tramples all over the family to express their desires without caring about everyone else's needs. However, a grown-up child grown under this narcissistic family will overreact and rise against as a message that no one should possibly perceive them in such a manner. Even though they might have led all their lives believing that their needs don't matter, they finally realize that either way, no one should walk over them just to meet their needs, but they always have the least idea on how to express it.

Zero self-confidence

The child grows into an adult who has zero confidence as this would have already been trampled on by the mother. They would never know how to speak up for themselves or defend themselves in whatever situation. This makes them vulnerable and has very low self-esteem. It starts simple, but things always start manifesting themselves into adulthood, and they cannot be confident enough in many circumstances.

Isolation from family

Most children grow up and isolate themselves from family, as they associate family with what their mother did to them. This becomes evident when you find that they leave home and never come back or never attend any essential family functions. They start new lives out of home and ensure they have cut ties with their family members. It becomes tough to begin convincing an abused child to be close to his family, as they always remember what they have been through. Unless they intentionally take it upon themselves to fix what has been broken, there is never a way to repair the damage.

Financial problems

Most children with narcissistic mothers have a hard time managing their finances, as they are used to having everything controlled by their mothers. They either become selfish and will not spend a dime on many things, or become spendthrifts because they try to make up for the chances they never had to spend their money without being controlled. They will not be able to know how and when to plan for their finances.

Crushed Self-Esteem

This is because the narcissistic mothers teach the children that they are worth nothing, right from birth. All your wants and needs mean nothing to the narc, and this naturally leads you to wonder why you're not getting them met. It must be because you're not worth it, you conclude.

Lost Sense of Self

Chances are your narc of a mother always told you who you were as you grew up. She sculpted you entirely in the image she preferred. You don't even know what you like or don't like when it comes to mundane things like ice cream flavors or music genres. You get to discover things you never realized about you. For a change, you get to be all about you, definitely not in the same way your mother was all about herself. You know what I mean.

Zero Confidence

Or near zero. The fact is this is something that plagues every child who had a narcissistic parent raising them. You find you're not so confident, no matter where you find yourself. Even when you're alone, you're somehow judging yourself. Since you're always used to being judged by your mother, you do the same to yourself and expect it of others.

Inability to Assert Yourself

Since you're not that confident, it's not a stretch to see why you can't assert yourself when you need to. Each time you tried to argue yourself with your mother, what you got instead was Now that you're all grown, you still do not assert yourself.

Terrible Relationships

You might find yourself drawn to narcissistic lovers and narcissistic friends. I know this indeed was the case for me. Now I'm a lot more discerning, thankfully. This means you can be, too. The reason you keep drawing narcissists to you is that's what you learned as you grew up.

Concealing Emotions

You learned as a child that you should not show your emotions. You're not allowed to be angry;

you're not allowed to be hurt. You'd better not indicate that you're either of these things while your narcissistic mother is abusing you. Did you scrape your elbow? Is it bleeding terribly? Too bad. You were also not allowed to express your joyous emotions.

Problems with Addiction

Children of narcissistic mothers often will develop one addiction or another as a coping mechanism for all the feelings that they have kept locked away on the inside. Society may turn its nose up at addictions, but the truth is they do have their use. They let you bear stuff you simply would not be able to, otherwise. While the addiction may have started as an innocuous solution, as the habits latch on, they become serious problems. Rather than criticize and condemn addicts, it would be better to find ways to help them deal with the emotions that they have buried instead.

Disjointed Thoughts and Emotions

It's difficult for you to know your true feelings about circumstances in your life. You don't even know what your thoughts are about a given situation. You're so used to believing that you cannot trust your own point of view. You're so used to looking to your narcissistic mother to tell you what to think and how to feel.

Unwillingness to Stake Your Claim

Growing up with your narcissistic mother means you were all about fulfilling her needs. You learned very quickly to ignore your own needs because if you didn't, you'd get into trouble for it. You were programmed to believe that getting your own needs met was incredibly selfish, and you ought to be ashamed of that. Something to consider now you're an adult is what true selfishness is. When you're selfish, you make things that are not about you to revolve around you.

Overachieving and Underachieving

With the children of narcissistic mothers, it usually pans out one of two ways. It's either the child decides to do all they can to prove themselves, to finally feel good enough. So they become overachievers, or they are continually sabotaging themselves, frequently having problems with finances, always failing because deep down they do not feel deserving of good things. The overachieving sort may sound like the better deal, but the truth is that they pay a steep price. The people in their lives who matter the most to them end up suffering as a result.

Social Anxiety

You wonder if you're too quiet or too loud. You wonder if you should have gone with red instead of blue. Where no one else can see, you carry a heavy load of shame deep down. You're ashamed of yourself. You're ashamed of who you are. You're worried that no one will love you. As a result, you find yourself creating a reality in which no one likes you, and that becomes a self-fulfilling prophecy. It's not because you're not the right person, or you're not sweet. It's because somehow others can tune into what we think of ourselves on a subconscious level, and they reflect you what you think.

Never Simply Accepting Compliments

This is a particularly common side effect of being raised by a narcissistic mother. Usually, it's because the few times she ever complimented you, it was followed by something to cut you down. When another person would complement you, she would be quick with a cutting remark.

Depression

Children of narcissistic parents are often prone to depression. It's sad but true. There's no surprise that this happens. You want to make connections with others, but are scared, or don't know how, or can't trust. Your self-esteem is almost nonexistent, thanks to dear old mom. You don't have the skills you need to move forward in life. You're always being criticized by your mother, despite your best efforts and intentions.

Being Suicidal

With all that depression and the reasons behind it, it's natural that you would have thoughts of ending it all or even have made several attempts.

Notes:

Narcissistic Mothers

Narcissistic Mothers

Chapter 9: (CPTSD) Complex Post-Traumatic Stress Disorder

There are kids of narcissistic mothers that have barely survived the psychological battle that came up during and after the nasty experience. We have seen children that have starved themselves to death just because that was the only way they could get away from the pain and hurt.

Having been trapped from childhood, they become victims of a mother that was incapable of showing them the kind of love that they wanted.

The narcissistic mother takes over the psychological aspect of the kid right from the time he gets born. Her lack of empathy and coldness will affect the kid from the beginning. The mother wants to experience the child not as a unique individual but rather as an extension of their lives.

The mother will sabotage your efforts to become a separate individual that is productive. She is envious of you on each level and will do everything to make sure you don't get ahead in life. They feel that gnawing feeling to compete with you at all levels, even when it comes to romance.

But you don't have to lead the life that she subjects you to – with the right approach, and you will heal from all the abuse.

Consequences of Narcissistic Abuse

Narcissistic mothers are all over, and they hide under various masks that they wear. You shouldn't get fooled or fall under their command because the results are often wrong. Behind the layer of confidence is a deeply insecure person who feels that the only sense of entitlement they have is over other people.

Whether you have a chance of getting out of an abusive relationship of you have been stuck with an abusive parent, you need to get away from leaving the stable.

One of the consequences of this form of abuse is complex post-traumatic stress disorder (CPTSD). Let us learn how it manifests and what it entails, and how you can deal with it.

What Is C-PTSD?

While you might have heard of the term post-traumatic stress disorder (PTSD), C-PTSD is also a real condition, and it can affect all areas of your life, including the way you relate with other people.

When you have C-PTSD, it shows that you are a survivor. The symptoms aren't a sign of illness or some form of weakness; instead, they just show that the mind and the body are attempting to cope with what you went through under the narcissistic mother.

C-PTSD is a relatively new diagnosis that was just included in the classification of diseases in 2018. It was initially categorized as a subset of PTSD.

C-PTSD has been defined as a disorder that might develop when you have been exposed to a series of events that are horrific or threatening in nature. The events need to be repetitive or prolonged and from which it is hard to escape. One of the most common causes of this condition is narcissistic abuse.

Statistics show that between 7 and 8 percent of Americans suffer from C-PTSD at one time or another in their lives. The main contributory factor to getting C-PTSD is PTSD.

Chronic trauma from narcissistic abuse is a major cause of the condition. And when a child is exposed to it, it ends up affecting the psychological development of the brain, which makes it harder for you to self-regulate emotions and then maintain stable relationships.

Often, the child believes that the parent will not abuse them, but since it has happened, then it compromises the ability for them to feel safe and trust other people that are around them.

When judging whether it is C-PTSD or another condition, all the diagnostic requirements for PTSD are usually met. However, in addition to the diagnosis for PTSD, C-PTSD is characterized by:

- Issues with affect regulation.

- A diminishing in the beliefs about oneself.

- A feeling of defeat or worthlessness that is then accompanied by feelings of guilt, fear, and shame often related to the event that happened

- A hard time sustaining romantic relationships and attitudes towards other people.

These symptoms end up causing various impairments to the family, personal, educational, social, and occupational and many other vital areas of functioning.

The condition usually comes up when there is a severe event or a life-threatening series of events that will put the brain's control center in high alert, which in turn throws the nervous system into a continuous state of fear.

The symptoms arise due to the changes that occur in various regions of the brain which deal with memory, emotion, and reasoning.

The main difference between PTSD and C-PTSD is how the trauma is developed, and the symptoms that come up after the trauma.

C-PTSD affects all kinds of people, regardless of gender, age, and race. Even the young kids that have been traumatized end up showing signs of developing C-PTSD. They will start having issues with speech and bedwetting. They might even re-enact the trauma during the playtime sessions with their peers. Currently, statistics show that women are more likely to develop C-PTSD as compared to men.

Diagnosis of C-PTSD

For you to be diagnosed with C-PTSD, you also need to meet the diagnosis of PTSD. This is a disorder that can develop following exposure to a horrific event or a life-threatening one. Or a series of life-threatening events.

For the diagnosis to stand, the following symptoms need to persist for a few weeks and then cause significant impairment in family, personal, occupational, educational, or any other area of functioning.

The symptoms come in various forms:

People with C-PTSD often struggle with intense and frequent symptoms of anxiety. They usually relieve the struggles they went through, and this makes them anxious most of the time.

When they relieve the trauma, they end up with flashbacks to what happened before, memory blanks, and nightmares. All that they are going through is a feeling that they are experiencing the trauma all over again.

When these victims have these symptoms, they will have intense physical sensations that come up due to the effect.

The reminders to the trauma can be in the person's thoughts, a place, people, or anything that will trigger the memory. Once the mind is triggered, the person feels like he or she is right in the event.

Dissociation

Trauma makes the person feel as if they don't belong to their own body, and their mind isn't there at all. They feel as if they are in a dream – the world around them isn't real at all.

Avoidance

C-PTSD makes the person feel as if they don't want to be associated with the trauma at all, so they keep away from situations that will remind them of what happened before. They will try to push away the memories that pop into their mind and will avoid places or people that remind them of what happened.

Fear

Since you have been in a situation that left you afraid of the people and the world around you, you end up feeling scared and always on the lookout for danger, you will still be jumpy and on edge even long after the trauma is over. The fear might prevent you from studying, sleeping, and also concentrating correctly.

A Negative Sense of the World

C-PTSD survivors usually have an overwhelming feeling of guilt, shame, and worthlessness. They blame themselves for what happened and will feel as if the world is against them when, in the real sense, the narcissistic mother is the one that brought about all these bad feelings.

Relationship Problems

C-PTSD makes it hard for the victim to be in a stable relationship for long. They will have shorter relationship patterns that don't make any sense to them. This is because they experienced a lot of abuse from the people that they thought would protect them, and they also went through betrayal that stayed with them.

They Don't Manage Emotions

Since their emotions haven't been necessary when they were growing up, they end up experiencing uncontrollable and intense emotions that will range from hate to rage to sadness to fear.

Wounded Self-perception

C-PTSD heap a lot of blame on themselves for the suffering that they go through. Feelings of shame and guilt usually tear them, and they might feel helpless and worthless to manage their lives and overcome the troubles that they are going through.

Have Little Faith

These C-PTSD victims have little or no faith in the world, the people, in themselves, and religious doctrines. They are usually pessimistic and cynical; they don't trust anyone and will view any kindness that they come across with a lot of suspicions.

Hyper Vigilance

Just because they perceive the world as if it is full of malice, they will be observing other people as well as other elements in the environment, continually looking for signs of danger and clues that someone has a bad intention that might harm them.

How Does C-PTSD Affect Relationships?

When you get exposed to severe trauma for a long time, it becomes hard for you to form intimate, safe, and secure relationships. The memories are so much embedded into your brain that it affects the way you view yourself and others.

A Negative View of Yourself

When you suffer from C-PTSD, you often struggle with feelings of shame and self-hatred. You end up feeling unworthy and damaged, such that you think you don't deserve any form of kindness or love from other people. This makes it hard for you to experience emotional intimacy, especially in relationships.

The person fears that they will be rejected when people know that they have undergone traumatic situations in life. They push other people away at the slightest provocation, and they need up feeling unacceptable and alone, thus reinforcing a negative self-view.

A negative View of the World

When you have suffered for long under abuse from a mother, then you will have a negative view of the world at all times. You will not have faith in yourself, and you feel that God doesn't love you at all.

C-PTSD will make you continuously change beliefs with the main aim of searching for security and love. This creates a lot of difficulties in your relationships.

Failure to Regulate Emotions

People that suffer from C-PTSD don't possess the skills to regulate their emotions. You will never be able to control your feelings the way other people do. They have been taught not to show their feelings and have learned to hide them till they slide away.

This makes these people hard to live with. You will keep them at a distance because you want to stay away from their emotionless lives.

Lack of Trust

People that suffer from C-PTSD have a huge struggle when it comes to trusting the people that they love.

The person with C-PTSD usually doesn't have a sense of trust even with the kids. No relationship works well with the person because they don't extend trust, so they cannot receive any trust from the kids. They feel isolated, and this leads to a case of abandonment.

Treatment for C-PTSD

While the condition can be handled in an outpatient setting, the aftercare is usually a vital process of healing from the C-PTSD. Treatment often begins in a residential treatment center where you have the full attention of mental health treatment specialists.

The period of these therapies ranges can be variable, and you will be in a supportive environment where the treatment will be provided as a priority for you.

The therapy will include supplementary medication as well as medication, life skills, and holistic management techniques. You will attend classes that will help you to understand the disorder much better as well as the causes of the condition.

The symptoms can be debilitating and can lead to chronic emotional silence. The good thing is that when you have compassionate, caring, and expert treatments, the symptoms are easy to manage, and the life-changing effects can be controlled easily.

When you seek out treatment for C-PTSD, you will wonder whether a therapist can be helpful for you. There are many things that you need to consider when selecting a therapist. Some of the practical issues include cost, location, and what kind of insurance the therapist accepts.

The therapist you approach needs to explain what the therapy entails, the duration of treatment, and when to know if it's working or not. Let us look at various ways you can choose the best therapist for your condition.

Thank you again for choosing Narcissistic Mothers. I hope you will find it. I would like to hear your thoughts with a short review on Amazon

Notes:

PART THREE: RECOVERING FROM A NARCISSISTIC MOTHER

Chapter 1: Protection Tips

Cut Down the Time You Spend Around Her

If your mother cannot change, and you learn that the abuse does not seem like it will ever stop, keeping your distance may be a logical step. However, you need to have come to terms with everything on your end. Merely preventing your distance from your mother won't work if you still have issues of your own to deal with. The effect of abuse is more emotional than physical and can follow you anywhere you go.

Keep Conversations Civil

In a civil relationship, you can choose to have less contact with your mother or have a friendly relationship with her rather than cutting off all contact. What this implies is that you limit your conversations to non-serious topics. You also don't make any attempt to get emotionally close to her. This is ideal if you have accepted that your mother will never show you love or empathy, but you want to keep communication still.

Get a Good Support System

Regardless of how old you are, getting a reliable support system can make a living with your narcissistic mother bearable. If you are a grown adult, you can get support from your friends and spouse. However, if you have kids, don't use them as therapists. This is no different from what a narcissistic mother does to her kids and can end up affecting them negatively in the long-run.

See Her as a Third Party and Not Your Mother

When you think of a mother, what comes to your mind is an appealing individual who would do anything to ensure your well-being. For this reason, it can be very confusing when they act completely different from what you would expect. In addition to confusion, this can cause you a considerable amount of anger as well.

If you want to stop seeing them as what they are not, and keep getting confused and angry, you need to change the way you view them. Instead, categorize her as just another woman who is not your mother. This way, you will begin to see the relationship you share for what it is.

Set Up Your Boundaries

Normally narcissistic mothers do not respect any of your boundaries. They cross them at will and feel no remorse. But this only goes on because you don't understand your boundaries yourself.

Instead, set up boundaries for yourself and understand when they are not being respected. Setting up these boundaries is only half the battle as you need to learn to make them stick, and respect these boundaries yourself. Creating boundaries is something only you have the power to do. If you discover the right way to go about this, it can be beneficial to both your long-term physical and mental health.

Sticking to Your Boundaries

A true narcissistic mother may try to manipulate you and cross these boundaries. She may call you unexpectedly even though you asked her not to, and drop-by at your workplace. Depending on the kind of narcissist she is, she may even feign illness in a bid to get your attention. Your job is to ensure you don't fall for any of her antics, as this is the best way to ensure your boundaries stick. If she leaves you angry messages or tries to guilt-trip you, don't take the bait. Instead, ignore her. The same goes if she calls you. If it becomes excessive, you can receive her calls and let her know once more how serious you are about it all.

Take Charge

After a while, many children with narcissist parents understand that they are being abused. They know that the lives they are living is not an ideal one but don't know how to make the change. Instead of waiting for someone to help you out with your situation, you need to be the best version of yourself.

Understand That Moving On May Be the Logical Option

If you are faced with a narcissistic mother, remember that there are many people in the same shoes as you. Find support online via support groups, articles, and other close friends. If you do decide to leave your narcissistic mother and move on, the next section will show you ways to achieve this.

Reduce the Current Conflict

If you want to regain your self-confidence, then you need to keep your mother at arm's length and then reduce the level of conflict between the two of you to a bare minimum.

You can choose to only respond to the right messages and then ignore any other abusive ones that she will send. When you ignore her, she will realize that the game is over, and the confrontations will be minimal. If you are grown-up, you can get a job out of town so that you avoid the daily confrontations that you have grown accustomed to.

Focus on YOU

When it comes to abuse, you will realize that your mother didn't want anything good to happen to you, so she made sure you instead focused on her needs and forgot yours.

Now is the time to try and please yourself rather than other people. Turn your priorities into self-care and then pamper yourself. If for the past years, you had been a slave to your mother, it is now time to be a slave to yourself.

Surround yourself with positive vibes from your friends to your community. Make sure you treat yourself to a good massage, go for daily exercise, eat well and meditate. You can also get some good quality sleep.

Tell the Truth

When you feel you are ready, you need to tell people the truth about yourself and where you had ended up. You will be shocked that people will get surprised at what you tell them. They will ask you why you hadn't told them the truth earlier so that they could assist.

Many people feel embarrassed to say what they had undergone, and for how long, they fear the backlash that will get to their mother. Since this is a woman that gave birth to you, you must disassociate yourself from her before you can move ahead.

Be Responsible

You will still receive abusive messages from your mother when she realizes that you are moving on without her. When you do, you need to maintain your focus on the journey ahead and become the best you can be for your own sake. When you are responsible, you won't be drawn into justifying your worth or defending what you do and how you do it.

Rebuild Your Life

All along, your life has been in shambles because of the abuse. This is the time you need to start building your life right from scratch. It might be a hard task, but we have had people that have done it the right way.

You need to find who the real you are and then make sure you become it. You can use online manuals and life coaches to find your real worth so that you can focus more energy on building yourself up instead of giving in to your conniving mother.

Work with a Counselor

When you are trying to make a change, there are a lot of people that will help you to succeed, but none as important as a counselor. The counselor will help you get ahead with your change and will give a listening ear.

You might find it hard to get the same help from a friend or a family member because they don't understand what you are going through. The professional will give you time to discuss what you have experienced and then learn the various ways to overcome the pain of the past.

Focus on the Positives

You will feel confident if you know how valuable you are in life. You need to make sure you focus on the good things that are happening in your life – you have an excellent education, a good husband, and a great job. You have a loving family, and you are in good health.

You need to come up with a list of what makes you unique and then place a spotlight on these things in your mind. If possible, you need to write down the positive traits and then put them at a point that you can check them out always.

Find Closure

For you to move on from a narcissistic abusive relationship with your other, you need to get some closure. The source of the closure depends on the nature of the relationship and the type of abuse that you have gone through all these years.

Start by forgiving the person that abused you for their actions. When you hold onto anger, you end up hurting yourself even more, and you will fail to move on in life. When you hold onto the anger, you make the abuser feel more powerful.

Moving out of the home and then disassociating yourself from negative aspects of your former life will assist you in moving onto a great experience that is waiting for you.

Don't Live in denial

After you have gone past the abuse and you have exposed it, you need to acknowledge it instead of living in presence. Many people pretend that the abuse never happened, and they end up hurting themselves the more.

For you to get away from the pretense, you need to integrate all the bad things that happened to you without letting the situations define who you are. This requires you to go through a serious paradigm shift and rewrite your history entirely.

You Have to Repair the Broken Bonds

This is one of the toughest tasks that you will face, especially when you denied that the abuse happened and you kept on defending your abusive mother while everything was happening.

When you side with an abusive person, you damage critical relationships. And even though the family and friends might not be so supportive, you might not be aware of how far their pain extends.

When you are recovering, you might not be burdened with the issue when you are on the road to recovery. Some of the relationships that you spoilt might never recover the closeness and the intimacy that they had, especially if you pushed them away.

When you restore broken relationships, you will get a support system of people that believe in you. They will help you recover your lost dignity and make you a hero again.

Learn to Identify Red Flags and Respect Them

Red flags are any sign that indicates a relationship is not ideal for you to be in, and they are always true indicators of what you can expect in the future. When you see a red flag arise in any relationship and you are a part of it, it is a sign to stop pursuing that relationship. You should always respect red flags because they never lie.

Reinforce Your Independence

Another thing you need to do to start protecting yourself is to reinforce your independence. Continually work on building up your self-confidence, self-esteem, and self-worth through fostering healthier relationships with yourself and with others. The more you can increase your sense of self and your independence, the more you will be able to rely on yourself and trust in yourself. This way, you are less likely to leave yourself exposed to the abuse of anyone in the future.

Plan What You Will Do?

You have a clear way to protect yourself, and you are not going to be left alone, confused, and trapped again. This is not your childhood and this person is not your guardian: you do have the right to say no. You terminate any relationship for any reason, including one relating to abuse or toxic behaviors. That includes your relationship with your mother if you ever find yourself in the abuse cycle again and in need of an escape plan.

Notes:

_____
_____
_____
_____
_____
_____
_____
_____
_____
_____
_____
_____
_____
_____
_____
_____
_____
_____
_____
_____
_____
_____
_____
_____
_____
_____
_____

Narcissistic Mothers

Chapter 2: Separation from a Narcissistic Mother

If you're going to become your true self and whole at last, then you need to cut your narcissistic mother off. No, it's not dramatic. It's merely the truth. You need to psychologically separate yourself from your mother if you're going to get to know yourself and understand your emotions. You can be on your own, without her. You can withstand whatever criticisms she has to throw at you. You can deal with the criticism you'll get from others for distancing yourself from your mother. When you give yourself time to get to know who you are, you'll find that you can be okay, whether or not you and your mother are in the same room.

No Contact

Having no contact doesn't mean it is temporary. It means leaving for good and not looking back, ever. Many people don't like the term no connection since it can easily be misconstrued as just temporarily not having communication. The bad news is narcissists are like cancerous tumors. They have to be removed entirely and swiftly from our lives. If this tumor isn't removed quickly, it could spread or grow into different organs. There are times when we have to cut all ties forever. This no contact phase is like rehab for the victims of narcissistic abuse. You have to have complete isolation to cleanse yourself of the narcissistic energy.

Saying goodbye is having the ability to completely let go of this toxic individual without having second thoughts or guilt. You don't have to follow them on social media, be their friend, or check in on them. Severing all ties is the only way you can move forward after being in a relationship with a narcissist mother. Having a relationship with narcissists mothers is an addiction that has been confused with love. When you are in rehab, you have to make sure you have complete isolation from all drugs to get back control of your life. It is essential to have a support system with family and friends.

If your insurance covers behavioral health, you need to make an appointment with a psychologist as quickly as you can after the relationship has ended. Therapy will help you with self-esteem and find the reasons why you let them abuse you.

What to Expect When You Break Up with Your Mother

When you cut ties with your mother, it is very rarely the case that you will be able to keep the relationships you have with the rest of your family. It's basically like you're a tumor, and you've had to excise yourself. She will make sure of it with her smear campaigns and the ultimatums she will issue to the rest of your family to choose aside.

It's not the final cure. Going no contact will allow you room to breathe, discover yourself as a person, heal, and grow. It won't stop your mother from smearing your name or trying to manipulate you from afar. It also won't cure the hurt inside. You need to work on recovery, and you could also use the services of a mental health professional to help you get better for good.

You'll feel even worse. But only for a short time. It makes sense that you should feel relief instead, but that's not the case for most children of narcissistic mothers. There's the fear of being isolated, and the fear that you've made a terrible mistake. You doubt yourself. Your mother has got her hooks in your head. Wait it out. The feeling will pass.

You need to work on recovery and healing. I cannot overemphasize how vital therapy is. You need to heal from the abuse from your mother, as well as heal from the harmful coping mechanisms you taught yourself. You don't need those crutches anymore. A professional therapist can help you get rid of them for good, so you can finally soar.

Expect some blowback. You're free now, but that doesn't mean your mother is done with you. You might get lucky. Perhaps your mother decides to punish you by blanking you out of existence. In her mind, she thinks she's hurting you when she's only helping you.

You might feel alone and misunderstood. Don't be surprised when your closest friends or even your partner does not support you on your decision to go no contact.

All that guilt and shame. It's not unusual for you to second guess yourself after you go no contact, to wonder if your mother is right about you being overdramatic and sensitive. You might also ask yourself if you're doing the wrong thing, ignoring your obligations to your mother. You feel guilty and ashamed.

Feelings of loss. When you break up with your mother, you'll feel like you no longer belong to your family. You might be surprised by the intense feelings which come up. You might even find yourself trying to patch things up with your mother. For some daughters, as they deal with the loss, they also realize how much better their lives are.

You've got to mourn. Your losses need to be mourned. You need to grieve. This ties in with acceptance, which we talked about earlier.

You may go back to your vomit. It happens. You might suddenly want to see if things have changed with your mother. You may have forgotten why you cut her out. If you give in, and you go back, and you find she is still who she is, please forgive yourself and begin again.

Trying to handle an extreme and unhealthy narcissist mother isn't easy, whether you decide to stay in their lives or walk away.

If you decide to walk away and cut ties, the way you handle this move is essential to consider. If your narcissist mother isn't abusive, being considerate and empathetic will make sure you can leave feeling good about your decision. Just keep in mind that narcissist mothers can't empathize at times, and this is because of heightened sensitivity. If you can let them down easy without exposing or confronting them, this might be the best thing to keep their self-esteem from suffering a massive blow. If abuse is present in the relationship, you have to cut the ties quickly or in a safe way that is expedient for you.

If your Narcissist Mother Returns

Just like any person who has been involved in a relationship, your narcissist mother will probably try to contact you. They could be suspicious, angry, or hurt about why you aren't in their lives anymore, depending on them and the relationship. This is understandable.

If you decided to quit talking to your parents since their actions were damaging to your well-being, their parental love isn't going just to disappear. Some people claim that narcissists don't love, but this isn't the case. They just can't show or express their love in front of other people. Some narcissists mothers find they have loving feelings emerge when they aren't around their narcissistic supply.

They could contact you in a rational manner that is caring, to celebrate, or in an attempt to get you back or get something from you. Every situation, just like every individual, will be different. If at all possible, to respond to these attempted contacts, please remember to have empathy, but deliver it in a way that doesn't invite doubt, questions, or hope. Stand by what you know is best and be firm instead of being open to the things they might offer you.

If you left a relationship you had with an emotionally abusive narcissist, you might find they will get in touch with you in the future. You should refuse contact instead of trying to reason or discuss things with them. No good will ever come from these interactions, just more harm. If they continue to contact you, and get angry, abusive, or emotional, not reacting might force them to gain control of themselves and move on.

If you have taken some distance from a family member who isn't abusive but has unhealthy narcissistic tendencies, you might receive an opportunity to have a conversation. This doesn't mean you will be opening yourself up for danger but says you are trying to be present in their lives as long as they can behave themselves. If they still can't act, you might have to figure out if you want to increase distance or continue the relationship.

Believe in Your Power

Before anything else, you need to believe in the power you have; it is your choice to make, and this decision is not beyond you. Over the years, you may have been made to feel insignificant. You may also believe that you have no power to take the best steps of your life. Remember that this is not true, and the power lies inside you. Leaving the one you grew up with is never easy, but you can do it, so long as you believe in yourself.

The Right Time

The moment you have gotten a bit of clarity and started to feel your self-confidence rising, then you may want to take this step and let go of the relationship. But you need to know that leaving your narcissistic mother behind won't be an easy task, as there may be a lot of battles to win if you want to get your way.

Understand That Your Health Is Paramount

It is understandable for many children to want to remain even with the abuse being meted out to them by their narcissistic parents. Since they have been conditioned to place the desires and needs of their narcissistic mother above theirs, it is usually a behavior that is hard to shake.

Come to Terms That Your Narcissistic Mother Won't Make It Easy

Of course, your narcissistic mother won't respect your decision to leave. For many narcissist parents, children are possessions and extensions of them. To them, they are not meant to have any personal desires. Your narcissistic mother probably sees you the same way and would do everything in her power to ensure you don't leave.

Be Prepared to Fight Guilt

Throughout the entire process of cutting off your mother, you will have to battle with a lot of guilt. This means you need to be prepared if this is going to be a success. There is a massive chance that over the years, you may have learned to feel guilty for everything, even when it is for your good. This is usually a way the narcissistic mother manipulates you into doing her bidding.

Notes:

_____
_____
_____
_____
_____
_____
_____
_____
_____
_____
_____
_____
_____
_____
_____
_____
_____
_____
_____
_____
_____
_____
_____
_____
_____
_____
_____
_____

Chapter 3: How to Heal from Narcissistic Abuse

Healing from any sort of abuse is difficult. However, you will be able to overcome the abuse you faced in your life and fully start to heal. There are many forms of violence, such as physical, emotional, psychological, and sexual. Unfortunately, narcissistic mothers can cause you to experience all these forms of abuse.

You should also realize that if you were every physically abused, you were also emotionally and psychologically abused. In many cases, any type of abuse will lead to emotional and psychological abuse. These are some of the hardest forms of violence to heal from because its effects are generally unseen. In fact, you can push the events into your subconscious mind that you don't even realize you are dealing with the effects of abuse.

There are several ways to heal from narcissistic abuse. The steps you choose to take are dependent on you and your personality. You might feel more comfortable following some of these steps over others. This is perfectly fine. Once you start making this change in your life, pat yourself on your back, be proud of yourself. Your healing journey has just begun.

Understand You Are Not Alone

Many people suffer in silence when they continue to struggle with any abuse they endured as a child or continue to face as an adult. Being silent about your struggles will only continue to hurt you. Some people went through the same type of abuse you did as a child and continue to deal with it as an adult. They have gone through the same emotions ranging from embarrassment to anger. While you can know and think that you are not alone, you will indeed find a sense of solidarity once you start meeting people and share stories. Narcissistic mothers also need to understand that they are not alone. There are also support groups, therapy, and many other ways to jumpstart your healing process.

Acknowledge Your Feelings

Another big step to healing is acknowledging your feelings. This can be tough for you because your mother most likely refused to acknowledge your feelings. She might have even told you to stop feeling in a certain way. This is because your emotions were a direct threat to her and would take the spotlight away from her. The only emotions which mattered to your mother were her own. To keep the focus on herself, your mother probably shamed or ridiculed you.

Because your mother pushed your feelings aside, she never taught you how to handle them. Therefore, you need to learn how to manage them in other ways, such as attending therapy or seeking the help of a trusted friend. When you acknowledge your feelings, you understand that they exist and are there for a reason. It is essential to know that your emotions never went away; you simply stopped listening to them. So, open up your mind to your feelings. Start understanding why you feel a certain way, why you think the way you do, and what makes you the person you are.

Emotions are a very powerful force within us and can often control the way we act and think.

When you start feeling attuned to your emotions, you will find yourself in a lot of emotional pain. You might begin to remember events that occurred when you were a child, which you placed into your subconscious mind and left there. However, it is essential to take this step, as you will begin to discover who you are truly. You will learn to handle your emotions, which will give you better control of your life overall.

Forgiving Yourself

Forgiveness is a big step toward healing from narcissistic abuse or causing the abuse. No matter what side of the coin you are on, you will struggle when it comes to forgiveness. However, it is essential to work toward it if you want to start building a healthy relationship.

First, I want to take the time to tell you that you can forgive. You can forgive your mother for her actions, and you can forgive yourself. If you are the mother, you can forgive yourself for everything you have done because of your personality disorder. There are various steps you can both take to start working toward forgiveness.

This won't be an easy road, and it can take years to forgive someone. However, with every step you choose, you will be one step closer to letting go and adding another building block on your healthy relationship.

Meditate

Meditation is a strategy that can help you overcome some of the biggest challenges in your life. When you are struggling with your past, you will notice that your thoughts are often negative. You feel stressed out and may feel like you lack control over your life. These are often ways that children of narcissistic mothers feel as they are some of the most common consequences.

Many people feel that meditation is a great tool to implement when you are looking to create calmer in your life.

Meditation will help ease your anxiety as it creates a sense of calm in your mind. With meditation, you will be able to focus on thinking clearer thoughts. For example, instead of thinking about losing your job, you will think about when you were in a previous situation and how well it worked out. You recall your supervisor being understanding and granting an extension because they know how hard you work on a project.

Ask Yourself Who You Are

Self-inquiry is an essential focus for people as you need to know and understand who you are. When a narcissistic mother raises you, you struggle with your self-identity for several reasons. This can be because you were never allowed to do what you wanted to do. You couldn't pick out your clothes, play the school sports you wanted, nor could you hang out with your friends. You always had to focus on your mother before yourself. Once you can let go of these factors and move forward, you can discover who you are.

Heal Your Inner Child

Your inner child is who you were. It is your inner child that stores your childhood memories, whether they are good or bad. If you have any lasting issues from your childhood, it is your inner child who is latching on to them. Therefore, to start healing yourself from a narcissistic mother, you will need to focus on improving its source, which is your inner child.

Your inner child is influenced by the situations you went through, events that took place, words that someone told you, the decisions you made, and other factors. Necessarily, each of these is pieces of your childhood, which helped mold the person you are today. Not every part of our inner child is something inside our conscious memory. Sometimes, it is in our subconscious mind and is triggered when we are in the middle of a particular situation or through therapy.

You know your inner child is wounded through the consequences you face from growing up with a narcissistic mother. The signs include low self-esteem, not knowing who you are or what you want to do with your life, lacking trust in yourself and other people, relationship struggles which include intimacy with your significant other, and being a bully or a rebel. Other signs can be emotional issues, such as anger, anxiety, depression, and being passive-aggressive.

Know You Will Recover

While it is a long and painful process, you will be able to manage the effects of your childhood. You might always remember some of the pain, you will always have the memories, and you might not ever fully forgive, but you will be able to find a way to manage. It is essential to know that you won't overcome the effects as if they never happened. Instead, through the strategies we have previously discussed, you will begin to heal and take your first steps into recovery.

Recognition

Before you can recover and heal from abuse from your narcissist parent, you need first to recognize the abuse. Like we previously stated, narcissistic abuse is subtle and can go unnoticed for many years. This is why many abuse victims don't even know there is abuse, especially when it involves psychological and emotional abuse.

You need to understand this and accept the situation for what it is. Stop hoping your mother will transform into someone compassionate. Accept the fact that your mother will never love you and will never care about your well-being. She will only show you love and affection so long as you do her bidding.

Be Aware of Your Feelings

Because your narcissistic mother must have abused you in numerous ways, you may have to get past feelings of anger and hurt to find yourself. As you know, narcissists are known to dump their blame and emotions on others. So, during the search for your true self, you may not quickly determine what you feel and what was dumped on you by your narcissistic mother. As you start to understand how to get accustomed to your feelings once more, remember not to judge yourself. Instead, determine your sympathies, recognize them, and respect them.

Let go of Past Experiences

Abuse is not something that happens in a day. It continues for years and sometimes lasts throughout the lifetime of the individual. Even if you are unable to remember them, these memories are stored somewhere in our minds and can influence the way we react to situations.

To heal, you would have to let go of all these experiences. A great way to achieve this is to pen down all of the skills you can remember. Also, write down how your narcissistic mother made you feel, and include everything you would have loved to say to her.

Once you are done, read through once more, squeeze this paper and burn it. This is a symbolic way of releasing your pent up feelings and freeing yourself from these experiences. Make sure you carry out this process continues until you feel a sense of freedom in your body.

Let go of the Self-Blame

This remains the same, even when you had nothing to do with the situation. A great way of eradicating the effect of your toxic mother in your life is to stop the whole self-blame. This can ensure healing is more seamless for you.

Keep a Journal

By now, you must know that writing things down has a way of helping you heal. This is an excellent option if you do not want to visit a therapist or can't afford one. Keeping an online or offline journal can accelerate your recovery process.

Write down everything that makes you angry; those things you were never able to voice out, all of your experiences, and the various forms of abuse and manipulation you were subjected to. These are emotions that you must have been keeping inside for a long time and ignoring. Doing this lets you feel them and make your peace with them. With this, you can genuinely and better understand yourself.

Take it as a Learning Experience

Looking back at all of the efforts you channeled into trying to make your mother love you, it can seem like you wasted a considerable part of your life. If you allow yourself, you can dwell on this and fail to make progress. This is understandable, but it is not the right way to go.

As opposed to looking at it as time you have wasted, look at it as a learning experience. The lessons you picked up all through the abuse can pave the way for personal growth.

Take Charge of Your Life

Narcissists like to control their victims and make them do all of their biddings. If you had a narcissistic mother, this was most likely your situation. You may have grown accustomed to living for her instead of yourself. Your priority is to ensure she is happy at all times, and you do so to the detriment of your desires.

To keep up your journey to recovery, you need to separate from your narcissistic mother. However, separation here does not have to do with the physical. You have to sever the mental connection you have made with your mother. As you know, narcissists project their emotions on others, so over the years, your mother must have projected many of her feelings into you.

Learn to Love Yourself Once More

Typical humans love themselves. However, due to your dysfunctional family, you have grown to believe that you are everything that is wrong with the world. This feeling is notably worse if you played the role of a scapegoat.

You need to break all of the illusions about yourself that must have developed from the constant insults and criticism. You are not flawed, and you are not crazy. You deserve love like everyone else, especially from yourself. Take an in-depth look into yourself and let go of all of these illusions. See the world as it should be and learn to love yourself once more.

Therapy

When it comes to therapy, you'll find that there are three parts to it. First, you must understand the background of the issue you're dealing with, get a firm grasp on the history of it, as well as what the diagnosis is. Second, you've got to address the emotions which are connected to the history head-on. Finally, you've got to create a new perspective from which you will look at life and living.

When it comes to narcissistic injury, it is not enough to simply "get over it" and move on. It's not enough to simply do affirmations, or reason and rationalize your way out of the pain you feel.

Stages of Grief for Children of Narcissistic Mothers

In the process of healing from narcissistic injury, we make use of the same stages of grief, except that there is a need to put acceptance in the number one spot.

Acceptance. You must first be accepting of the fact that your mother is incapable of love. She does not understand empathy and has none to give. The reason you need to be accepting of this is quite simple. If you do not accept this fundamental truth about your mother, then you will simply not be able to work your way out of the haze of denial that you have been living in all your life.

- Denial. It's merely that the only way you could have handled that truth was to deny it. As a child, there is nothing that matters to you more than the love of your mother. When you don't get it, you feel out of place.

- Bargaining. All your life you've been bargaining with your narcissistic mother and with yourself on her behalf as well. You've

227

spent the whole time wishing, hoping, praying, and believing that she will change for the better, sooner or later. You keep telling yourself that she is going to love you, as soon as you do this, achieve that, change this, or that. You tell yourself that one of these days, she will actually show up for you when you need her.

•Anger. At this point, you're stark raving mad at your mother. You realize that she never designed to cater to your emotional needs as a child. She neglected you, time after time. She took your tragedies, your despair, and turned them into opportunities to have the spotlight on her. You get really angry, full of rage, even, when you realize that you had allowed her to treat you like this.

•Depression. In this phase, you feel a sadness that is beyond words. It's not even accurate to say it's a sadness. It's like there's a black hole inside of you, and it just sucks up all the joy and light in your life. You feel terrible because you realize that you've got to let go of whatever dreams you had of your mother, finally being the mother you've always wanted. You feel like an orphan. You finally release every single expectation and hope that you've held on to so desperately all this time. You are depressed because you realize your dreams about you, and your mother's relationship will never be.

Understand What Narcissism Is

The best way to begin to acknowledge the personality disorder is by understanding what Narcissism is. One of the biggest challenges that someone who struggles with a personality disorder and someone who doesn't often come across understands the personality disorder. This goes for both people involved. If you believe you could be a narcissistic mother, it is hard to acknowledge that you could have a personality disorder. If you are the child of a narcissistic mother, it's hard to recognize that your mother has a personality disorder. However, this is one of the most crucial steps when it comes to healing for both parties.

Understand You Are Suffering

Not only do you need to understand Narcissistic Personality Disorder, but you should know that you are suffering as a consequence of it. Unfortunately, you are likely suffering from the after-effects of being raised by a narcissist more than you realize. Of course, you will be able to heal. However, you need to identify how you are suffering to overcome them.

Ignoring a Narcissistic Mother

When you need to save your life and lead a better one, you need to learn to ignore the abusive mother. And there is no better time to ignore her than when she tries to punish you.

The narcissistic mother will always love to see how you react, and when they know that you are acting the way they wanted, you end up giving away your power.

This is how the narcissistic mother prospers – she likes to know that she has transcended your thoughts, heart, mind, and everything you own to the point where they mean everything to you in all ways.

Accept that she Won't Change

Many victims of abuse think that their mother will one-day change and become the loving mother that they thought they had – wrong.

Tune into Your Feelings

As the child of a narcissistic mother, you have been tuned to ignore any feelings that come your way. You have been made to hate or even fear them. The mother feels that when you have feelings, you will try to react to her.

The best thing you can do as a person dealing with a narcissist is to try and connect with your feelings. If they have been made dormant, then you need to awaken them so that you can feel what you need to.

Create healthy boundaries

Though achievable, setting healthy boundaries between you and the narcissist person is always not an easy task, especially if the person is a close family member such as a parent. This first step is to design a strategy. If there is a long-standing array of other people violating your borders, then changing this and taking things to standard will not be easy. Identify all the potential goals and obstacles that will count for you to achieve success.

Don't take things too personal

Narcissists are always in denial of their mistakes, cruelties, and shortcomings to protect themselves from feeling shame or inferior. They achieve this by projecting their faults to those around them. This can be very upsetting being blamed for something you didn't do or being classified with negative traits that you don't even possess.

Look for support and purpose somewhere else

A narcissist will not simply change into another version that values and loves you and, in this case, you will need to seek personal fulfillment and emotional support elsewhere. Learn the components of a healthy relationship.

Living with a Narcissistic Mother

After you identify that the person suffers from NPD, you need to look for ways to get what you need in terms of safety and to ignore the negative issues that come with the mother. Take time to know what manipulative techniques the mother uses, and then come up with strategies to combat them.

You need to look at the family and find out what sort of support you have. When the other members of the family have your back, you will be able to make things work for you, but if you find that they side with the abuser, then you need to make sure you find a way to handle issues on your own.

This is your mother that we are talking about and remember that you need to make sure you maintain the family bond that exists. Take time to find a way to make things work, but don't get hurt in the process.

When you have the right to support people and a therapist to assist you, you will be able to make things work for you. Make sure you get the right person to help you handle the issues that come with abuse.

Notes:

_____
_____
_____
_____
_____
_____
_____
_____
_____
_____
_____
_____
_____
_____
_____
_____
_____
_____
_____
_____
_____
_____
_____
_____
_____
_____
_____

Narcissistic Mothers

Narcissistic Mothers

Chapter 4: Self-Healing Tips

Here are the tips towards self-healing a survivor of a narcissistic mother:

Understanding the Vocabulary is Empowering

One of the best ways to heal from this form of abuse is to try and understand the terminology that is used in an abusive form of narcissism. When you know the language, you will be able to read professional articles well and be able to understand various aspects of abuse, including emotional flashbacks, gaslighting, word salad, attachment styles, C-PTSD, stonewalling, stages of recovery and other concepts. You will also understand the clear definitions, as well as have precise examples that will make it easy for you to understand what is going on.

Get into a Routine

Routines are not only important for children but also adults as well. For example, in the morning, you might get up, start the coffee pot, take a shower, get dressed, have a cup of coffee while you are reading your morning devotions, or simply listening to the quiet of your home. You might then take a few minutes to meditate before you walk your children to school and finish getting ready for your day. In the evening, you might find that you sit up and read for an hour after putting your children to bed, take time to write in your journal, and then watch an episode of your favorite television show.

Stay Away from Things That Cause Your Negativity

It would help if you always remembered the gravitation effect when you are trying to maintain a positive mindset. This means that if you know something makes you frustrated, angry, sad, or causes you to think negatively, you need to stay away from this as much as possible. While these are a couple of the most popular social media platforms people use, they are often filled with negativity.

Reframe Your Thoughts

To reframe your thoughts, you start by closing your eyes and taking a few deep breaths. As you do this, you will notice the noise becoming quieter, and you can think more clearly. You then start to think about everything good that is happening in your life. For example, you feel thankful that you didn't wake up any later. You feel grateful to have electricity so you can tell the time. You give thanks for the fact that your children are old enough to dress themselves with a little help from you. This helps you, as you can get ready at the same time. The more you start thinking positively about the situation, the happier you feel. Even though you still feel a little rushed, you also know that everything will be fine. Your children will get to school, you will get to work, and you will all go through your day just like any other day.

Listen to Music

Music is a significant step when it comes to therapy. You can work through nearly every emotion that you feel through a song or two. You will start feeling like you are not alone or that you can overcome the obstacles you face. Music can make you feel more creative, energetic, and give you something to focus on, which will allow you to change your mindset about a situation.

Make Sure You Are Getting Enough Sleep

People often forget how important sleep is. People will often sacrifice sleep to stay up later to get more "alone time" or finish watching a movie they are interested in. Just because you are an adult doesn't mean that you can thrive on three to four hours of sleep every night. While this might be okay for a couple of nights, you will quickly find yourself struggling to get through your day, think clearly, or remain productive. This is because when you lack sleep, you start feeling sluggish, you have trouble focusing on tasks, and you find yourself thinking negatively.

Never Be Afraid to Ask for Help

Many people struggle with asking other people for help. There are several reasons for this, especially for someone who grew up with a narcissistic mother. One reason is that you lack trust when it comes to other people. Therefore, you aren't sure if they will truly help you or if they have another agenda, such as trying to get you to owe them a favor. Another reason is that whenever you asked your mother for help, she would respond by yelling, ignoring you, or even telling you something negative such as you are not worthy of support or helping you is a waste of time.

Count Your Blessings

When many people need to focus more on creating positive thoughts, they will often start thinking about everything they are grateful for. This can be their family, friends, home, vehicle, animal companions, education, groceries, and savings account. When you count your blessings, you don't need to think of everything you are grateful for and count them. This is essentially a figure of speech. It means that instead of thinking about what is going wrong in your life, you need to think about what is going right. Doing this will help you gain the best positive mindset that you can acquire.

You Always Have a Choice.

You need to know that even in those instances when the times seem bleak and you have nothing to do, there is always a choice that you can make. Even during those times when you are in unbearable anguish, you have a chance to beat the cycle.

However, the traumatized mind always tries to make sure your cognitive mind doesn't work at all. Immediately you start wondering what to do so that you can get into the good books of your mother.

Recovery is not easy

The complex trauma that arises from the abuse takes a long time to develop. This can be years, even a decade or more. It, therefore, comes naturally that healing doesn't happen instantly – it takes time. If you come across a therapist that promises to heal you in a few days, then look for another one.

Your mother took her time to chip away at your sense of self and spirit, which means that healing form this process will take time and is an ongoing process. You might not have complete freedom from the past, so you need to make sure that you have the right procedure to learn and then take the right steps.

Notes:

_____
_____
_____
_____
_____
_____
_____
_____
_____
_____
_____
_____
_____
_____
_____
_____
_____
_____
_____
_____
_____
_____
_____
_____
_____

Narcissistic Mothers

Conclusion

It is almost impossible to make your narcissistic mother love anyone but herself, and this includes you. She can only see people as little more than possessions. She lacks empathy and enjoys projecting her feelings onto others. Instead of trying to determine the areas of your life that are not perfect, channel your energy into healing from all of the abuse you have suffered over the years.

Time is of the essence when it comes to breaking free from this situation. Treating emotional damage left by years of narcissistic abuse can take a lot of time. The longer you wait, the more damage it will cause in your overall life. Do everything possible to heal and leave the effects of the abuse you have suffered behind.

If you feel your narcissistic mother is worth saving, then, by all means, try. Getting your life back together after suffering years of abuse is never easy, but that does not mean it is impossible. I have given you all of the tips and strategies that worked for me, and they can work for you too. All you need to do is read, digest, and implement all of the information in this book, and with time, you will undoubtedly get your life on track once more.

Now you know what she is, and you know what to do to free yourself of her clutches, heal, and move on with your life. However, knowing is only half the battle. Are you ready to act? Are you afraid? If you are afraid, it is understandable. It's also all the more reason you need to pull the trigger without thinking.

You can heal. Are you ready? Then seek professional help, and do what needs to be done. All survivors of narcissistic parenting will be rooting for you. You've got this.

Please stay consistent in your path and continue working toward your recovery every day, as it will take time for you to recover fully. Be patient with yourself, have compassion for yourself, and show yourself as much love as you can. Trust that you are doing your best in every moment and that your life will get better.

As you continue to move forward with your healing, be sure to continue educating yourself around what to expect, and surround yourself with people who can help you. The more informed you are, and the more supported you feel, the easier it will be for you to truly move beyond your mother's abuse and into your recovery. Keep building up your support system and leaning into them when you need to, and trust that they are there to help you. They care about you, love you, and want to see you succeed. There are genuine, kind people in the world, and you can and will find them and surround yourself with them.

I hope you had useful information by reading Narcissistic Mothers. Please let me know your sincere thoughts by leaving a short review on Amazon. Thank you.

Notes:

_____
_____
_____
_____
_____
_____
_____
_____
_____
_____
_____
_____
_____
_____
_____
_____
_____
_____
_____
_____
_____
_____
_____
_____
_____
_____
_____